Select Poetry

Chiefly Devotional

of

The Reign of Queen Elizabeth.

COLLECTED AND EDITED

FOR

The Parker Society,

BY

EDWARD FARR, Esq.

WIPF & STOCK · Eugene, Oregon

Wipf and Stock Publishers
199 W 8th Ave, Suite 3
Eugene, OR 97401

Select Poetry Chiefly Devotional of the
Reign of Queen Elizabeth
By Farr, Edward
ISBN 13: 978-1-60608-435-9
Publication date 01/07/2009
Previously published by
Cambridge University Press, 1845

Select Poetry

Chiefly Devotional

of

The Reign of Queen Elizabeth.

COLLECTED AND EDITED

FOR

The Parker Society,

BY

EDWARD FARR, Esq.

PART THE FIRST.

PREFACE.

ALTHOUGH some pieces of the religious poetry of the age of Queen Elizabeth have been often reprinted, its great variety and extent are known only to those who have made this department of literature their study. The object of this selection is to present to the members of the Parker Society specimens of the authors of that age who wrote sacred poetry: and it is hoped that the design is satisfactorily accomplished as far as can be expected in such a work.

In making the selection the Editor has kept in view the object for which the Parker Society was founded; that of exhibiting the principles of the Reformation, by the republication of the works of the Reformers, and their immediate successors; and it has been his aim to select pieces which are in accordance with those principles. In one or two instances, where the poems related to the Reformation, they have been printed entire; and the whole may be considered as an illustration of some of the results which the English Reformation produced on the literature of the age, and in the minds of the people at large.

Prefixed are very brief biographical notices of the writers in this collection. Of many of them so little is known, that the editor is only able to mention their names and the titles of their books.

It was found difficult to draw an exact line for guidance as to the writers to be included in the selection, from the uncertainty as to the precise period when some of the pieces were published. The desire has been to present poetry of the reign of Queen Elizabeth; but there are a few poems which may have first appeared a few years later. It has not been thought advisable to enter into disquisitions on the merits and characters of these writers. In the age in which they wrote, poetry was too often supposed to consist in the form rather than in the substance, and in the rhythm rather than in the matter. Notwithstanding, the reader will find very much in these pages that may be recognised as true poetry; while throughout the whole he will discern a purity of sentiment, with a devotional feeling which were characteristics of the age to which the volumes refer, and he will often find truly poetic ideas and vigorous thoughts beneath a rugged and even uncouth exterior.

PREFACE.

The old spelling has been retained, so that these pieces are literal reprints, except where obvious errors of the press have been corrected. Some obsolete words are explained in a Glossary at the end.

It was needful, on account of the rhyme and rhythm, to retain the original spelling and structure of the words; the Council of the Parker Society have done this in the present instance the more willingly, as it strongly confirms the propriety of the course they deemed it right to pursue with the prose writings of the Reformers, namely, to adopt a regular orthography, conformed to the usage of the present day, while the original words have been strictly preserved.

The selection has been derived from public and private libraries. The thanks of the Council of the Parker Society and of the editor are due to several gentlemen who have aided them in their design; but more especially to William Henry Miller, Esq., whose library in this department of English poetry is the richest in the kingdom. To Mr. Miller's kindness they are indebted for extracts from many rare volumes in his possession, several of which could not be met with elsewhere, and seem to be unknown to bibliographers. Mention must also be made of the kindness of the Rev. Thomas Corser, who obligingly contributed extracts from several rare volumes in his valuable library of Elizabethan poetry.

The best acknowledgements of the Council are also due to Mr. Pickering, Mr. Thorpe, Mr. Lilly, Mr. Stewart, and other booksellers, and especially to Mr. Rodd, for the ready kindness with which they have assisted the editor in his inquiries, and have in several instances allowed him access to rare volumes in their possession.

E. F.

IVER,
December 30, 1845.

CONTENTS.

		PAGE
PREFACE		v
Biographical Notices		ix
I.	Queen Elizabeth	1
II.	Archbishop Parker	2
III.	Edmund Spenser	6
IV.	George Gascoigne	33
V.	Barnaby Barnes	41
VI.	Sir Philip Sidney, & the Countess of Pembroke	53
VII.	Sir John Davies	86
VIII.	Fulke Greville, Lord Brooke	107
IX.	Sir John Harington	115
X.	Michael Drayton	116
XI.	Henry Lok	130
XII.	William Hunnis	143
XIII.	Thomas Bryce	161
XIV.	Sir Nicholas Breton	178
XV.	John Hall, M.D.	197
XVI.	Geffrey Whitney	203
XVII.	Humphrey Gifford	211
XVIII.	William Byrd	222
XIX.	Anthony Munday	226
XX.	Sir Walter Raleigh	233
XXI.	Abraham Fraunce	237
XXII.	John Davies	240
XXIII.	Thomas Howell	256
XXIV.	Thomas Tusser	257
XXV.	Richard Vennard	264
XXVI.	G. C.	266
XXVII.	J. Rhodes	267
XXVIII.	Francis Kinwelmersh	291
XXIX.	Richard Edwardes	295
XXX.	Arthur Bourcher	297

CONTENTS.

XXXI.	D. Sand	299
XXXII.	Lord Vaux	302
XXXIII.	Richard Hill	305
XXXIV.	T. Bastard	306
XXXV.	G. Gaske	307
XXXVI.	Candish	308
XXXVII.	William Bvttes	309
XXXVIII.	Anonymous	310
XXXIX.	William Samuel	312
XL.	T. Marshall	313
XLI.	M. Thorn	314
XLII.	Thomas Scott	315
XLIII.	Walter Devereux, Earl of Essex	316
XLIV.	Francis Davison	318
XLV.	Christopher Davison	332
XLVI.	Joseph Bryan	333
XLVII.	Richard Gipps	337
XLVIII.	T. Carey	338
XLIX.	George Whetstone	339
L.	Dudley Fenner	341
LI.	Stephen Gosson	344
LII.	Anonymous	346
LIII.	Samuel Rowlands	374
LIV.	E. W.	358
LV.	Ann Dowriche	359
LVI.	John Markham	361
LVII.	John Davies	363
LVIII.	Richard Robinson	364
LIX.	Edward Hake	368
LX.	Roger Cotton	372
LXI.	Leonard Stauely	376
LXII.	William Warner	377
LXIII.	Anonymous	381
LXIV.	Timothy Kendall	384
LXV.	Peter Pett	386
LXVI.	John Pits	387
LXVII.	G. B.	388
LXVIII.	Stephen Batman	389

CONTENTS.

LXIX.	William Broxup	390
LXX.	Barnaby Googe	391
LXXI.	Francis Sabie	393
LXXII.	Andrew Willet	394
LXXIII.	C. T.	395
LXXIV.	Henry Willobie	396
LXXV.	Samuel Daniel	397
LXXVI.	R. D.	399
LXXVII.	T. Proctor	400
LXXVIII.	Thomas Churchyard	402
LXXIX.	Michael Cosowarth	404
LXXX.	G. Ellis	408
LXXXI.	Elizabeth Grymeston	412
LXXXII.	Thomas Lloyd	415
LXXXIII.	Thomas Drant	417
LXXXIV.	R. Thacker	420
LXXXV.	Anonymous	422
LXXXVI.	Anonymous	434
LXXXVII.	Anonymous	447
LXXXVIII.	Henry Dod	449
LXXXIX.	James Yates	450
XC.	A. W.	452
XCI.	Anonymous	454
XCII.	John Bodenham	455
XCIII.	John Norden	459
XCIV.	Bartholomew Chappell	465
XCV.	Henoch Clapham	466
XCVI.	Christopher Fetherstone	467
XCVII.	John Marbeck	468
XCVIII.	Thomas Gressop	469
XCIX.	H. C.	470
C.	Charles Best	471
CI.	Anonymous	473
CII.	Anthony Fletcher	475
CIII.	Robert Holland	477
CIV.	H. C.	478
CV.	Thomas Sternhold	480
CVI.	W. P.	484

CONTENTS.

CVII.	John Hopkins	485
CVIII.	Thomas Norton	487
CIX.	William Whittingham	489
CX.	William Kethe	492
CXI.	Robert Wisdom	493
CXII.	John Pullain	495
CXIII	John Mardley	497
CXIV.	Anonymous	499
CXV.	T. B.	501
CXVI.	D. Cox	503
CXVII.	E. G.	505
CXVIII.	Anonymous	506
CXIX.	W. A.	508
CXX.	L. Ramsey	511
CXXI.	W. Elderton	512
CXXII.	Robert Burdet	514
CXXIII.	Jud Smith	516
CXXIV.	Gregory Scott	520
CXXV.	Christopher Lever	523
CXXVI.	John Phillip	525
CXXVII.	Thomas Middleton	534
CXXVIII.	John Awdelie	540
CXXIX.	Edward Wollay	541
CXXX.	William Gibson	542
CXXXI.	Anthony Nixon	543
CXXXII.	Abraham Fleming	645
CXXXIII.	Edmond Eluiden	547
CXXXIV.	Anonymous	549
CXXXV.	Thomas Nelson	551
CXXXVI.	Thomas Newton	553
CXXXVII.	Nicholas Boweman	554
	Memorial of Queen Elizabeth (CXXXL.)	556
	Glossary	557

BRIEF NOTICES

OF THE WRITERS IN THIS SELECTION.

I.

QUEEN ELIZABETH.

QUEEN ELIZABETH occasionally wrote sacred poetry. "Two little anthems, or things in metre of hir majestie," were licensed to her printer in 1578; and a copy of the 14th Psalm from her pen has been preserved. This literary curiosity occurs at the end of a book, entitled "A godly Medytacyon of the Christian Sowle, etc. compyled in Frenche, by Lady Margarete, Quene of Naverre." This psalm is reprinted in Park's edition of "The Royal and Noble Authors of Great Britain," and is the only fragment of her poetical remains adapted to these pages.

II.

ARCHBISHOP PARKER.

THIS eminent prelate of the English Protestant Church was a native of the city of Norwich. He was born in 1504, and was educated in Corpus Christi College, Cambridge. After he had taken orders, and during the reigns of Henry VIII. and Edward VI., he had various preferments bestowed upon him: of these he was deprived in the reign of Queen Mary; but when Elizabeth ascended the throne, he was consecrated archbishop of Canterbury. He died in 1575.

Before Archbishop Parker became primate, he executed a metrical version of the entire Psalter, either, as Warton remarks, "for the private amusement and exercise of his religious exile, or that the people, whose predilection for psalmody could not be suppressed, might at least be furnished with a rational and proper translation." This work was subsequently printed without date or translator's name, under the title of "The whole Psalter translated into English Metre, which contayneth an hundredth and fifty Psalmes. The first Quinquagene. Cum gratia et privelegio Regiæ Majestatis per decennium." The other two *quinquagenes* are indicated by half titles. Warton states that this translation was never published; and Strype says that he could never get a sight of it from its great scarcity. There are, however, copies extant in the Bodleian Library, the British Museum, and Lambeth Palace Library, beside others in private libraries.

III.

EDMUND SPENSER.

EDMUND SPENSER was born in East Smithfield about the year 1553. In 1569 he was admitted as a sizar of Pembroke Hall in the University of Cambridge, and he attained the degree of Master of Arts in 1576. In after life he became secretary to Arthur Lord Gray of Wilton, lord deputy of Ireland, who appears to have been his firm and bountiful patron; for the poet terms him "the pillar of his life." The chief occupation of Spenser's life, however, was literature, to which he was ardently attached to the day of his death, January 16, 1598—9.

The chief work of Spenser is his "Faerie Queen," the object of which is "to represent all the moral virtues, assigning to every virtue a knight, to be the patron and defender of the same; in whose actions the feats of arms and chivalry, the operations of that virtue whereof he is the protector, are to be expressed, and the vices and unruly appetites that oppose themselves against the same are to be beaten down and overcome." The "Faerie Queen" scarcely admits of extract, and Spenser is introduced into these pages chiefly as the author of two beautiful hymns on Heavenly Love and Heavenly Beauty. But the claims of Spenser to the title of Sacred Poet may be estimated as much by the titles of poetical treasures lost, as by those we possess. He wrote paraphrases of "Ecclesiastes," and of the "Canticum Canticorum;" the "Hours of our Lord," the "Sacrifice of a Sinner," and the "Seven Penitential Psalms," which are irretrievably lost to posterity.

IV.

GEORGE GASCOIGNE.

The time and place of the birth of this old English poet are unknown. His occupation was the profession of arms, and he was likewise a follower of the court of Elizabeth: we find that he accompanied the queen in one of her progresses. His poems are numerous, and of a miscellaneous character. In republishing his works Gascoigne thought proper to deprecate censure on the poetical levities of his youth; and the preface is thus addressed: "To the reuerende deuines unto whom these posies shall happen to be presented, George Gascoigne, Esquire, professing armes in defence of God's trueth, wisheth quiet in conscience, and all consolation in Christ Jesus." The religious poems of Gascoigne were evidently written in what he calls his "middle age," when he saw and lamented the follies of his youth. The original editions of his poems are among the rarest books in the English language. Gascoigne died in a religious, calm, and happy frame of mind, in 1577.

V.

BARNABY BARNES.

Barnaby Barnes was a younger son of Dr. Richard Barnes, bishop of Durham. He was born in Yorkshire, about the year 1569, and at the age of seventeen he became a student of Brasenose College, Oxford.

He left the university without a degree, and Wood says that he knew not what became of him afterwards. It appears, however, that in 1595 he accompanied a military expedition into Normandy, to aid the king of France, in which country he remained until 1594. Barnes wrote "A Divine Centurie of Spiritual Sonnets," which work issued from the press in 1595.

VI.

SIR PHILIP SIDNEY AND THE COUNTESS OF PEMBROKE.

SIR PHILIP SIDNEY and the COUNTESS OF PEMBROKE were the offspring of Sir Henry Sidney, of Penshurst, in Kent. Sir Philip was one of the most celebrated characters of his times. His popularity was great both at home and abroad. In his youth he attended both the universities; and when his education was completed, he visited different foreign countries. He spent a year in Italy, and on his return he was taken into favour by Queen Elizabeth. In 1586, Sir Philip accompanied a military force sent from England to assist the people of the Netherlands in throwing off the yoke of Spain. During this expedition he lost his life in a skirmish near Zutphen.

In this selection Sir Philip Sidney is introduced, together with his sister the Countess of Pembroke, as the joint authors of " The Psalmes of David, translated into divers and sundry kindes of verse, more rare and excellent, for the method and varietie, than ever yet hath been done in English." Manuscript copies of this version of the Psalms of David are to be found in the Bodleian Library, Oxford, and in the libraries of two or three private individuals. It is not certain which portions were written by Sir Philip and which by the countess; but the title-page of one of the MSS. in the Bodleian Library states that the version was "begun by the noble and learned gent, Sir Philip Sidney, Knt. and finished by the Right Honorable the Countess of Pembroke, his sister."

VII.

SIR JOHN DAVIES.

Sir John Davies, an eminent lawyer, was born in 1570, and died in 1626. His "Nosce Teipsum, or The Soul of Man and the Immortality thereof," from which the extracts in this volume are taken, first appeared in 1599, and it was dedicated to Queen Elizabeth.

VIII.

FULKE GREVILLE, LORD BROOKE.

Sir Fulke Greville, afterwards Lord Brooke, and on whose monument it is inscribed that he was "Servant to Queen Elizabeth, counsellor to King James, and friend to Sir Philip Sidney," was the author of several works, among which was one entitled "Cælia," containing CIX Sonnets, from whence those under his name are derived.

IX.

SIR JOHN HARINGTON.

Sir John Harington was one of the most noted characters in the reign of Elizabeth, as a courtier and a man of wit. His poems are chiefly of a secular character; but some few of his minor pieces have a moral and religious tendency, and among them are a few versions of selected psalms.

X.

MICHAEL DRAYTON.

This poet was born in 1563, and died in 1631. He enjoyed a high degree of popularity during his long life, and left a name still regarded with respect. His works are numerous, but the only volumes offering extracts suitable to these pages, written in the age of Elizabeth, are "Moyses in his Map of Miracles," and "The Harmonie of the Church: containing, The spiritual songes and holy hymnes of godly men, patriarkes, and prophets; all sweetly sounding to the praise and glory of the Highest." This latter work was published in 1591, and is not included in the editions of Drayton's collected poems.

XI.

HENRY LOK.

OF this author little is known, though he appears to have been connected with the court of Elizabeth, to whom he dedicated some of his pieces, comprising two hundred sonnets, treating of meditation, humiliation, prayer, comfort, joy, and thanksgiving. His name occurs to a small book in the Bodleian Library, entitled "Sundry Psalms of Dauid translated into verse, as briefly and significantly as the scope of the text will suffer." These Psalms are included in the very rare work which he published in 1597, entitled "Ecclesiastes, otherwise called the Preacher. Containing Saloman's Sermons or Commentaries—as it may probably be collected—vpon the 49 Psalme of Dauid his father. Compendiously abridged, and also paraphrastically dilated in English poesie, according to the analogie of Scripture, and consent of the most approued writers thereof. Composed by H. L., gentleman. Whereunto are annexed sundrie Sonnets of Christian Passions heretofore printed, and now corrected and augmented with other affectionate Sonnets of the same author's." In the whole there are 320 sonnets in the volume; those on "sundrie Christian Passions" comprising 200 of that number.

XII.
WILLIAM HUNNIS.

HUNNIS was a gentleman of the Royal Chapel under Edward the Sixth, and afterwards chapel-master to Queen Elizabeth. He was the author of "Certayne Psalmes chosen out of the Psalter of David, and drawen forth into English metre;" "A Handfull of Honeysuckles;" "A Hive full of Honey;" "Various Paraphrases of portions of Scripture History;" and "Seven Sobs of a Sorrowful Soule for Sinne, comprehending those Seven Psalmes of the Princélie Prophet David, commonly called Pœnitentiall." It is from these various works that the extracts in these pages are derived.

XIII.
THOMAS BRYCE.

THOMAS BRYCE appears to have been a clergyman: according to Ritson, an epitaph of "Mr. Bryce, preacher," was licensed to John Allde. He, however, escaped the rage of Queen Mary, and in 1559 he published "A Compendious Register in Metre, conteining the names and pacient suffryngs of the membres of Jesus Christ; and the tormented and cruelly burned within England, since the death of our famous Kyng of immortall memory Edwarde the Sixte: to the entrance and beginnyng of the raign of our Soueraigne and derest lady Elizabeth of England, Fraunce, and Irelande, quene etc."

XIV.
SIR NICHOLAS BRETON.

LITTLE is known of this poet, but Bishop Percy says he was of some fame in the reign of Queen Elizabeth. He is known to be the author of several works, and many are ascribed to him which appeared anonymously. Those from which the annexed specimens are derived are entitled: "A small Handfull of Fragrant

Flowers gathered out of the louely garden of Sacred
Scriptures, fit for any honorable or worshippfull gen-
tlewomen to smell to;" "An Olde Man's Lesson;"
"An excellent Poeme upon the longing of a blessed
heart: which loathing the world, doth long to be with
Christ;" "The Soule's immortall Crown; consisting
of seaven glorious graces. 1. Virtue. 2. Wisdome.
3. Love. 4. Constancie. 5. Patience. 6. Humilitie.
7. Infiniteness;" with a conclusion entitled *Gloria in
Excelsis Deo;* and a small volume of sonnets, entitled
"The Soule's Harmony."

XV.

JOHN HALL, M.D.

DR. HALL was a celebrated writer in the age of
Elizabeth on matters pertaining to anatomy and
chirurgy. He was also well known, in his day, as a
poet. His chief work, copies of which are extremely
rare, was published in 1565, under the title of "The
Court of Virtue: contaigning many Holy or Spretual
Songs, Sonnettes, Psalms, Ballets, and short sentences,
as well of Holy Scripture as others, with Musical
Notes."

XVI.

GEFFREY WHITNEY.

GEFFREY WHITNEY wrote "A choice of Emblemes,
and other Devises, for the moste parte gathered out
of sundrie writers, Englished and moralized, and
divers newly devised. A worke adorned with varietie
of matter, both pleasant and profitable: wherein those
that please maye finde to fit their fancies: Bicause
herein by the office of the eie, and the eare, the
minde may reape dooble delight throughe holesome
preceptes, shadowed with pleasand deuises: both fit
for the vertuous, to their incoraging; and for the
wicked, for their admonishing." From one of the
emblems in this volume, which was printed at Ley-

den in 1586, it appears that the author was a native
of Cheshire, it being inscribed, " To my countrimen
of the Namptwiche in Cheshire;" the wood-cut of
which represents a phœnix rising from the flames,
and the lines underneath allude to the rebuilding of
Namptwiche after a dreadful fire which consumed a
great part of it in 1593. Each emblem is illustrated
by a wood-cut. Thus the emblem, having for its
motto *Super est quod supra est*, which is here re-
printed, has a print representing a pilgrim leaving
the world (a geographical globe) behind, and travel-
ling towards the symbol of the divine name in glory
at the opposite extremity of the scene.

XVII.

HUMPHREY GIFFORD.

THIS author, of whom nothing seems to be known by
biographers, wrote "A Posie of Gilloflowers," which
was published in 1580.

XVIII.

WILLIAM BYRD.

WILLIAM BYRD was one of the "Gentlemen of the
Queene's Maiestie's honorable Chappell." In 1583 he
published a work entitled "Medius: Psalmes, Sonets,
and Songs of Sadness and Pietie," from which the
following specimens are derived. In the original
copies the poetry is set to music.

XIX.

ANTHONY MUNDAY.

ANTHONY MUNDAY, "servant to the Queen's most
excellent Majestie," published in 1588, "A Banquet
of Daintie Conceits. Furnished with verie delicate
and choyse inuentions, to delight their mindes, who
take pleasure in musique, and therewithall to sing

sweete ditties, either to the lute, bandora, virginalles, or anie other instrument." He was also the author of "The Mirrour of Mutibilitie," published in 1579, which describes the fall of princes and others, as recorded in Scripture. From these two very rare works the specimens in these pages are transcribed.

XX.

SIR WALTER RALEIGH.

CONSIDERABLE uncertainty prevails as to Sir Walter Raleigh's poetical productions, but that he was capable of producing poetry of a very high order, some pieces undoubtedly written by him abundantly testify. Among these are one or two hymns written during his imprisonment, which exhibit not only his genius, but the sincerity of his heart and the piety of his feelings.

XXI.

ABRAHAM FRAUNCE.

FRAUNCE was a poet of some note in the age of Queen Elizabeth; but nothing is known of him beyond the simple fact, that he published in 1591 a volume entitled "The Countesse of Pembroke's Yuychurch. Conteining the affectionate life and vnfortunate death of Phillis and Amyntas: that in a pastorall; this in a funerall; both in English hexameters;" and that to this was added a second part, entitled "The Countesse of Pembroke's Emanuel. Conteining the Nativity, Passion, Buriall, and Resurrection of Christ: together with certeine Psalmes of Dauid: all in English hexameters." The measure in which Fraunce wrote these productions was adopted by his contemporaries, Sir Philip Sidney and Richard Stanyhurst, but it is altogether foreign to our inflexible English language. Thomas Nash says of it: "The hexameter verse I grant to be a gentleman of an ancient house—so is many an English beggar;—yet this clime of ours he cannot thrive in : our speech is too craggy for him to set his plough in; he goes twitching and hopping like a man running upon quagmires, up the hill in one syllable and down the dale in another, retaining no part of that strictly smooth gait which he vaunts himself with among the Greeks and Latins." The specimen derived from this author's pages will illustrate the correctness of these sentiments.

XXII.

JOHN DAVIES.

JOHN DAVIES—usually called "John Davies of Hereford, to distinguish him from Sir John Davies—was a contemporary of Sir Philip Sidney. His poetical works are numerous: consisting of "Microcosmos," "*Summa Totalis*, or All in All, and the same for ever;" "The Holy Roode, or Christ's Cross: containing Christ crucified, described in speaking picture;" "The Muses' Sacrifice, or Divine Meditations;" "The Scourge of Folly;" "Humours Heau'n on Earth; with the ciuil warres of Death and Fortune;" "Witte's Pilgrimage, by poetical essaies, through a world of Amorous Sonnets, Soule's Passions, and other passages, divine, philosophical, and moral:" etc, etc. From these various works the specimens in this volume are derived.

XXIII.

THOMAS HOWELL.

THOMAS HOWELL wrote "The fable of Ouid treting of Narcissus, translated out of Latin into Englysh Mytre, with a moral thervnto, very pleasant to rede." This work was published in 1560, and the stanzas annexed to his name are extracted from the moralization.

XXIV.

THOMAS TUSSER.

THOMAS TUSSER wrote and published "Fiue Hundredth Pointes of good Husbandrie." The first edition was published in 1557, entitled "A Hundredth good Pointes of Husbandrie," but after passing through several editions it appeared in 1573, in an enlarged form, under the first-mentioned title. Tusser died in 1580. This work generally is not suited to these pages; but among the "manie other matters both profitable and not vnpleasant for the reader," mentioned on the title-page, are two poems which entitle the author to a place in this selection.

XXV.

RICHARD VENNARD.

VENNARD was a gentleman of Lincoln's Inn. He wrote "A Panegyric on Queen Elizabeth;" "The true testimonie of a faithfull and loyall subject;" and "The right way to Heauen." This latter work, from which our specimen is derived, was published in 1601.

XXVI.

G. C.

No mention is made of this author by Ritson. He wrote "A Piteous Platforme of an Oppressed Mynde set downe by the extreme surmyzes of sundrye distressed meditations." The work is written partly in prose and partly in metre, and it contains versions of five Psalms.

XXVII.

J. RHODES.

IN 1602 appeared "An Answere to a Romish Rime lately printed, and entituled, 'A proper new Ballad, wherein are contayned Catholike Questions to the

Protestant.' The which Ballad was put forth without date or day, name of authour or printer, libel-like, scattered and sent abroad, to withdraw the simple from the fayth of Christ vnto the doctrine of Antichrist, the pope of Rome. Written by that Protestant Catholike, I. R." These are the initials of J. Rhodes, whose very rare production is now presented to the reader in an entire form.

XXVIII.

FRANCIS KINWELMERSH.

This author was a member of Gray's Inn, and he and his brother Anthony had the character of being noted poets in the age of Elizabeth. They were the friends of George Gascoigne. His poems in this volume are from "The Paradise of Dayntie Deuises," which first appeared in 1576.

XXIX.

RICHARD EDWARDES.

Richard Edwardes was a native of Somersetshire, and born about 1523. In 1547 he was a student of Christ Church, Oxford, and in 1561 he was constituted a gentleman of the royal chapel by Queen Elizabeth, and master of the singing-boys in that chapel. In 1566 he attended the queen in her visit to Oxford: he died in the same year. Edwardes was one of the principal contributors to "The Paradise of Dayntie Deuises;" but only one of his poems is suitable to these pages.

XXX.

ARTHUR BOURCHER.

Arthur Bourcher is author of a poem entitled "Golden Precepts," which appeared in the edition of "The Paradise of Dayntie Deuises," published in 1600. Previous to this he published a fable of Æsop, versified, and he has a poem to the reader before Geoffrey Whitney's "Divine Emblems." Beyond this nothing is known of this author.

XXXI.

D. SAND.

This author was one of the contributors to "The Paradise of Dayntie Deuises." Some identify him with Dr. Sands, or Dr. Edwyn Sandys, archbishop of York, he being the only known author of this name and period: but the identification is not at all probable. Some of the poems in the above collection have the initials D. S. affixed to them, and they have been supposed to be by the same person who wrote those to which D. Sand is appended.

XXXII.

LORD VAUX.

Lord Vaux was one of the contributors to "The Paradise of Dayntie Deuises." On the back of the title-page to the edition published in 1580 he is styled "the elder," which refers to Thomas, second Lord Vaux, who was born in 1510. Ritson and others have suggested, however, that William, third Lord Vaux, who died in 1595, was a joint contributor with his father to that collection. The pieces ascribed to Lord Vaux are numerous.

XXXIII.

RICHARD HILL.

A writer of whom nothing is known beyond the fact, that he was one of the contributors to "The Paradise of Dayntie Deuises." Yet Webbe in his "Discourse of English Poetrie," published in 1586, speaks of his skill in many pretty and learned works, as he does also of D. Sands.

XXXIV.

T. BASTARD

WROTE, and published in 1598, "Chrestoleros: seven bookes of Epigrames." Many of these epigrams are addressed to the celebrated men living in the age of Elizabeth.

XXXV.

G. GASKE.

ONE of the contributors to "The Paradise of Dayntie Deuises." Nothing is known concerning him: Park thinks he may be identified with George Gascoigne.

XXXVI.

CANDISH.

PROBABLY Thomas Cavendish, Esq. the celebrated navigator, to whom Robert Parke dedicated his translation from the Spanish of "The Historie of the great and mightie kingdome of China," which was published in 1588. Candish was one of the contributors to "The Paradise of Dayntie Deuises."

XXXVII.

WILLIAM BVTTES.

WILLIAM BVTTES, of whom the editor has not met with any account, wrote "A Booke of Epitaphes," etc. which was published in 1583.

XXXVIII.

ANONYMOUS.

THE contribution of an unknown writer to "The Paradise of Dayntie Deuises."

XXXIX.
WILLIAM SAMUEL.

In 1569 appeared a work entitled "An Abridgement of all the Canonical Books of the Olde Testament, written in Sternhold's meter by W. Samuel, Minister." Beyond this nothing is known of its author.

XL.
T. MARSHAL.

One of the writers in the "Paradise of Dayntie Deuises."

XLI.
M. THORN.

One of the contributors to the "Paradise of Dayntie Deuises."

XLII.
THOMAS SCOTT.

Scott wrote "Four Paradoxes: of Arte; of Lawe; of Warre; of Seruice." This work, which was published in 1602, was dedicated to the Marquess of Northampton. No mention is made of this author by Ritson.

XLIII.
WALTER DEVEREUX, EARL OF ESSEX.

Walter Devereux, Earl of Essex, distinguished by his suppression of a rebellion in Ireland, and as the father of Robert Earl of Essex, has been pointed out as the author of "A godly and virtuous Song," extant in the Sloane MSS. No. 1898. This is printed in the "Paradise of Dayntie Deuises," having for its title "The Complaint of a Sinner," and with the initials F. K. affixed to it. These initials refer to Francis Kinwelmersh, and it is doubtful by which of these individuals it was written; but the Earl of Essex is supposed to have the fairest claim to the production.

XLIV.

FRANCIS DAVISON.

FRANCIS DAVISON was the eldest son of William Davison, who was secretary of state and privy counsellor to Queen Elizabeth. In 1602 he published "A Poetical Rapsodie, containing diuers Sonnets, Odes, Elegies, Madrigals, Epigrams, Pastorals, Eglogues, with other Poems, both in rime and measured verse." As a collection of Elizabethan poetry, this work has been always highly esteemed, and has gone through repeated editions. Davison, however, is introduced into these pages as one of the writers of "Divers Selected Psalms of David, in verse, of a different composure from those used in the Church," the MS. of which is among the Harleian Collection in the British Museum. Francis Davison was by far the largest contributor to this version of select psalms.

XLV.

CHRISTOPHER DAVISON.

CHRISTOPHER DAVISON was the second son of secretary Davison. Nearly all that has been ascertained about him is, that he was a member of Gray's Inn, and that he translated some of the select version of Psalms in the Harleian MS. mentioned under Francis Davison. The time and place of his death are unknown.

XLVI.

JOSEPH BRYAN.

OF BRYAN nothing more is known than that he wrote a few of the versions of the Psalms in the

Harleian MS. to which the Davisons were contributors. His name is prefixed to the Introduction to the manuscript.

XLVII.

RICHARD GIPPS.

OF GIPPS nothing more is known than that he has left versions of the first and second Psalms in the MSS. contributed to by the Davisons and Bryan.

XLVIII.

T. CAREY.

CAREY wrote Psalm cxi. in the select version mentioned in the preceding notices. This, however, is not found in the original MS., but in a copy, "Manuscrib'd by R. Cr." This manuscript is beautifully bound in white vellum, with other original poetry; the whole being entitled "A Handful of Celestial Flowers; viz. divers selected Psalms of David in verse, differently translated from those used in the Church; Divers Meditations upon our Saviour's Passion; Certain Hymnes or Carrolls for Christmas Daie; A Divine Pastorell Eglogue; Meditations upon the 1st and 13th verses of ye 17th chap. of Job. Composed by divers worthie and learned Gentlemen." The other poems in this MS. belong to a later date than that to which this selection refers.

XLIX.

GEORGE WHETSTONE.

WHETSTONE was a noted writer in the age of Elizabeth. His works in prose and verse are numerous: one affords a specimen for these pages. This was published in 1576, and is entitled "The Rocke of Regard: divided into foure parts: the first, the Castle of Delight; the second, the Garden of Vnthriftinesse; the third, the Arbour of Vertue; and the fourth, the Orchard of Repentance." It is from the fourth part of this volume that the extract is derived; the language of the whole of which is that of repentance for a life of folly.

L.

DUDLEY FENNER.

DUDLEY FENNER published in 1587, at Middleburgh, "The Song of Songs, that is, the most excellent Song which was Solomon's, translated out of the Hebrue into English Meeter with as little libertie in departing from the wordes, as any plaine translation in prose can vse: and interpreted by a short commentarie."

LI.

STEPHEN GOSSON.

STEPHEN GOSSON appears to have enjoyed considerable poetic reputation in the age of Elizabeth. By Francis Meres his name is mentioned in conjunction with that of Spenser; and Wood also bears testimony that he was celebrated "for his admirable penning of pastorals." Among other poems he wrote one entitled *Speculum Humanum*, which is printed in Kirton's "Mirror of Man's Life," which was dedicated to Anne Countess of Pembroke, and published in 1580. This latter poem is reprinted in these pages.

LII.

ANONYMOUS.

THIS author wrote a small poem, which consists only of a few leaves, entitled "The Loue of God." There is no date to it, but it bears internal evidence of having been written in the reign of Queen Elizabeth.

LIII.
SAMUEL ROWLANDS.

SAMUEL ROWLANDS was the author of a great many poetical works. Among them was, "The Betraying of Christ: Iudas in despair: with poems on the Passion," which was published in 1598.

LIV.
E. W.

THIS author wrote a poem entitled "Thameseidos, deuided into three bookes, or cantos," which was published in 1600. The lines extracted are from the close of the first canto.

LV.
ANN DOWRICHE.

ANN DOWRICHE wrote "The French Historie: that is, A lamentable Discourse of three of the chiefe and most famous bloodie broiles that haue happened in France for the Gospell of Iesus Christ, etc." This work was published in 1589, and at the back of the title-page are the arms of the Edgecombe family, after which follows the dedication, addressed to her "loving brother Master Pearse Edgecombe, of Mount Edgecombe in Deuon." Between this dedication and a prose address to the reader are some stanzas, which, as the pious composition of a lady, possess interest. They form an acrostic to her brother; each stanza commencing in every line with one letter of his name.

LVI.
JOHN MARKHAM.

IN 1600 a work was published entitled "The Teares of the Beloued: or, The Lamentation of Saint John concerning the Death and Passion of Christ Jesus our Saviour. By J. M.," that is, John Markham.

LVII.
JOHN DAVIES.

Two of this name appear before in this selection, but this John Davies has not been identified with either of them. He wrote "Sir Martin Mar-people: his coller of esses," from the close of which the extract under his name is derived. The work was published in 1590. No mention is made of his work by Ritson.

LVIII.
RICHARD ROBINSON.

RICHARD ROBINSON was the author of a volume entitled "A Golden Mirrour: conteyning certaine pithie and figurative visions prognosticating good fortune to England and all true English subiects. Whereto be adioyned certaine pretie poemes written on the names of sundrie both noble and worshipfull." This work was published in 1589.

LIX.
EDWARD HAKE.

EDWARD HAKE was educated under John Hopkins, the metrical associate of Sternhold, and afterwards became an attorney in the Common Pleas. He was the author of several prose and poetical works, and among others the following, from which the specimens of his poetry are derived. 1. "Newes out of St. Powle's Churchyard." 2. "A Commemoration of the most prosperous and peaceable Raigne of our gratious and deere Soueraigne, Lady Elizabeth, by the grace of God, of England, Fraunce, and Irelande, Queene, etc. now newly set foorth this xviii day of Nouember, beying the first day of the xviii yeere of her Majestie's sayd raigne, 1575." 3. "Of Gold's Kingdome and this vnhelping age. Described in sundry poems intermixedly placed after certaine other poems of more speciall respect, etc." 1604.

LX.

ROGER COTTON.

ROGER COTTON wrote "A Spirituall Song: containing an historicall discourse from the infancie of the world untill this present time;" and "An Armor of Proofe brought from the Tower of Dauid to fight against Spannyardes, and all enimies of the trueth." The former of these works was published in 1595, and the latter in 1596.

LXI.

LEONARD STAUELY.

LEONARD STAUELY, of whom no mention is made by Ritson, wrote "A Breef Discovrse wherein is declared of ye trauailes and miseries of this painful life, and that death is the dissoluer of man's miserie." There is no date: but it is supposed to have been published about 1580.

LXII.

WILLIAM WARNER.

WILLIAM WARNER wrote "Albion's England: a continued Historie of the same Kingdome, from the Originals of the first Inhabitants thereof: and most the chiefe alterations and accidents there hapning vnto, and in the happie raigne of our now most gracious Soueraigne, Queene Elizabeth. With varietie of inuentiue and historicall intermixtures." This elaborate poem, which exhibits a view of the secular and ecclesiastical events in English history, was first published in 1592. It scarcely admits of extract, but the stanzas here given may shew the talent of the poet, and the nature of his poetry. The ninth book is devoted to the exposure of popery and the horrors of the Spanish Inquisition.

LXIII.

ANONYMOUS.

This author wrote "The Passions of the Spirit," which was published in 1599.

LXIV.

TIMOTHY KENDALL.

Timothy Kendall, who was educated at Oxford, and afterwards became member of Staple's Inn, wrote "Flowres of Epigrammes out of sundrie the most singular authors selected: to which is annexed, Trifles deuised and written for the most part at sundrie tymes in his yong and tender age." The date of the publication is 1577.

LXV.

PETER PETT.

Peter Pett wrote "Time's Iourney to seeke his daughter Truth, and Truth's letter to Fame," which was published in 1599.

LXVI.

JOHN PITS.

John Pits wrote "A Poore Man's Beneuolence to the afflicted Church," to which are added two Psalms. This work was published in 1566.

LXVII.

G. B.

G. B. wrote "A New Booke called, The Shippe of Safegarde." This work was published in 1569. Ritson refers these initials to Barnaby Googe, and Bernard Garter; but it is not certain that they can be identified with either.

LXVIII.
STEPHEN BATMAN.

STEPHEN BATMAN, professor in divinity, was a native of Bruton in Somersetshire: he died in 1581. Batman was the author of several prose and poetical works, among the latter of which is, "The trauayled Pylgrime, bringing newes from all partes of the worlde, such like scarce harde of before." This work was published in 1569.

LXIX.
WILLIAM BROXUP.

WILLIAM BROXUP, of whom, as well as several others in this collection, no mention is made in Ritson, wrote "St. Peter's Path to the Joyes of Heauen, wherein is described the frailtie of the flesh, the power of the spirit, the labyrinth of this life, Sathan's subtilitie, and the soule's saluation." This work appeared in 1598.

LXX.
BARNABY GOOGE.

BARNABY GOOGE was a celebrated translator in the reign of Queen Elizabeth; he wrote some original works, among which is a work entitled "Eglogs, Epytaphes, and Sonettes," which was published in 1563.

LXXI.
FRANCIS SABIE.

FRANCIS SABIE was the author of some sacred poems entitled "Adam's Complaint: The Old Worlde's Tragedie: Dauid and Bathseba," which appeared in 1596. He was the author also of some secular works in hexameters and blank verse.

LXXII.

ANDREW WILLET.

ANDREW WILLET was a learned divine. His works, which are numerous, are chiefly prose. Among his poetical works is one entitled *Sacrorvm Emblematvm*, which is written in Latin and English. There is no date affixed to it, but it was written within the reign of Queen Elizabeth.

LXXIII.

C. T.

WROTE "A Short Inuentory of certayne Idle Inuentions; the fruites of a close and secret garden of great ease, and little pleasure." This work was published in 1581.

LXXIV.

HENRY WILLOBIE.

WILLOBIE was the author of a work entitled "Avissa: or the true picture of a modest maid, and of a chast and constant wife:" it was published in 1594.

LXXV.

SAMUEL DANIEL.

SAMUEL DANIEL was born in 1562, and was educated at Magdalen Hall, Oxford. He became tutor to Lady Anne Clifford, subsequently Countess of Pembroke, to whom several of his works are dedicated. The poetical productions of Daniel are numerous, and the tenor of his writings is generally moral and instructive; but only one, his "Musophilos," which contains a general defence of learning, affords extracts suitable to this selection.

LXXVI.

R. D.

R. D. wrote "An Exhortation to England to ioine for defense of true religion and their natiue countrie." There is no date affixed to this work, but it bears internal evidence of having been written in the age of Elizabeth.

LXXVII.

T. PROCTOR.

The extract from this author is from "The Gallery of Gallant Inuentions, edited by and contributed to by T. Proctor," which was published two years after "The Paradise of Dayntie Deuises;" namely, in 1578.

LXXVIII.

THOMAS CHURCHYARD.

Thomas Churchyard was a celebrated writer of prose and poetry in the age of Elizabeth. His works are chiefly of a secular character. The first specimen in these pages is transcribed from "A Mvsicall Consort of Heauenly Harmonie, compounded out of manie parts of musicke, called Chvrchyard's Charitie." This work appeared in 1595, and was dedicated "To the Right Honorable Robert Deverevx, Earle of Essex." The "Verses fit for euery one to knowe and confesse" are an extract from a rare work in Lambeth Palace library, entitled "The Wonders of the Air:" date 1602. Churchyard contributed one of the poetical translations to the Old Version of Psalms.

LXXIX.
MICHAEL COSOWARTH.

MICHAEL COSOWARTH wrote a version of some select Psalms, which is among the MSS. in the Harleian Collection at the British Museum. Complimentary verses are prefixed to this work by Richard Carey and Henry Lok, or Locke.

LXXX.
G. ELLIS.

THIS author wrote a poem, now very rare, entitled "The Lamentation of the Lost Sheepe."

LXXXI.
ELIZABETH GRYMESTON.

THIS lady was the daughter of Martin Barney, or Bernye, of Grimston, in Norfolk, and married Christopher, the youngest son of Thomas Grymeston, in the county of York. She wrote "Miscellanea: prayers, meditations, memoratiues;" in which there are seven "Odes in imitation of the seuen Pœnitentiall Psalmes, in seuen seueral kinde of verse."

LXXXII.
THOMAS LLOYD.

THE selected stanzas from this writer are transcribed from a work published in 1592, entitled "Evphves' Shadow: the battle of the dances, wherein youthfull folly is set down in his right figure, and vaine fancies are prooued to produce many offences."

LXXXIII.

THOMAS DRANT.

THOMAS DRANT, who was more memorable as a preacher than a poet, wrote "A Medicinable Morall, that is, the two Bookes of Horace his Satyres; Englyshed according to the prescription of Saint Hierome. The Wailyngs of the Prophet Hieremiah, done into Englyshe verse. Also Epigrammes." This book was published in 1566, being "perused and allowed accordyng to the Quene's Maiestie's iniunctions."

LXXXIV.

R. THACKER.

THE "Godlie Dittie" written by this author is here reprinted from the Harleian Miscellany.

LXXXV.

ANONYMOUS.

IN 1601 was published "The Song of Mary the Mother of Christ; containing the story of his life and passion; the teares of Christ in the garden; with the description of the heauenly Ierusalem." This work was issued anonymously, and the principal poem in it bears a strong resemblance to that entitled "Mary Magdalen's Lamentation for the Losse of her Maister Jesus."

LXXXVI.

ANONYMOUS.

THIS author wrote a volume entitled "Mary Magdalen's Lamentations for the Loss of her Maister Jesus," which has been supposed by some to be the production of Sir Nicholas Breton.

LXXXVII.

ANONYMOUS.

In 1597 a work was published, entitled "Saint Peter's Ten Teares. Ten Teares of S. Peter's, supposedly written vpon his weeping sorrowes for denying his Maister Christ." These Teares are preceded by a metrical introduction: they are ten small poems, each consisting of six stanzas of six lines.

LXXXVIII.

HENRY DOD.

In 1603 Henry Dod published a small volume of "Nine of the Singing Psalms," which he turned "into easie meter," for the use of his own family "and some godly learned friends." At a subsequent date he issued, with the royal privilege, "Al the Psalmes of Dauid, with certene Songes and Canticles of Moses, Debora, and others, not formerly extant for song." Beyond this nothing is known of this author, except that Wither, in his "Scholler's Purgatory," calls him a "silkman."

LXXXIX.

JAMES YATES.

In 1582 was published "The Castell of Courtesie, whereunto is adioyened the Holde of Humilitie, with the Chariot of Chastitie thereunto annexed: also a Dialogue between Age and Youth, and other matters herein contained. By Iames Yates, seruing-man." Besides the principal subjects which are enumerated in the title-page, this volume contains a great variety of minor poems.

XC.

A. W.

THIS writer was one of the contributors to Davison's "Poetical Rhapsody." The only names agreeing with the initials, mentioned by Ritson, are Andrew Willet and Arthur Warren, and he is inclined to attribute them to the latter; but no proof exists. Sir Egerton Brydges' supposition, that the poems to which they are affixed were by Sir Walter Raleigh, is equally unsupported. The author lived after the death of Sir Philip Sidney, in 1585: he wrote an eclogue, an epigram, and some hexameters upon his death.

XCI.

ANONYMOUS.

ANOTHER of the contributors to Davison's "Poetical Rhapsody."

XCII.

JOHN BODENHAM.

JOHN BODENHAM is not introduced into these pages as a poet, but as the compiler of "Belvedere, or the Garden of the Muses; which is a collection of sentences from most of the principle poets, living and dead, which are arranged in the form of poems." An address to the reader is prefixed, in which there is a statement of the authors from whose works the extracts have been made; but the extracts are so arranged as to make them appear as the original compositions of the compiler.

XCIII.
JOHN NORDEN.

The works written by this author from which the specimens are derived, are, 1. "*Vicissitudo Rerum:* an Elegiacall Poeme of the interchangeable courses and varietie of things in this world," which was published in 1600; and 2. "A Progress of Pjetie, or the Harbour of Heauenly Harts, etc.," first printed in 1596. Both these works are prose, interspersed with poetry.

XCIV.
BARTHOLOMEW CHAPPELL.

This author wrote, "The Garden of Prudence; wherein is contained a patheticall Discourse and godly Meditation, most brieflie touching the vanities of the world, the calamities of hell, and the felicities of heauen." The title-page continues, "You shall also find planted in the same diuers sweet and pleasant flowers, both necessarie and comfortable both for body and soule." This work, which is in prose and verse, was inscribed to Ann Countess of Warwick. It was published in 1595.

XCV.
HENOCH CLAPHAM

Wrote "A Briefe of the Bible's Historie: drawn first into English poesie, and then illustrated by apt annotations: whereto is now added a Synopsis of the Bible's Doctrine." This work was first published in 1596, and, although a very small volume, it displays great biblical knowledge. It is chiefly prose, and the prose far transcends the poetry in merit. The stanzas selected, which exhibit a brief view of Christianity, may serve as a specimen.

XCVI.

CHRISTOPHER FETHERSTONE

TRANSLATED "Christian and Wholesome Admonition, etc.," in which the piece of poetry annexed to his name is found. The work was published in 1587.

XCVII.

JOHN MARBECK.

JOHN MARBECK was organist of St. George's Chapel, Windsor. He wrote "The Holie Historie of King Dauid, drawn into English meetre for the youth to reade," which was published in 1579.

XCVIII.

THOMAS GRESSOP.

THOMAS GRESSOP was of All Souls' College, Oxford. He was a man of learning and piety. In the reign of Edward VI. he was chaplain to the army against Scotland; and in the reign of Elizabeth, a reader of divinity in the university, and a preacher at Saint Paul's. The stanzas annexed to his name were first published in the folio edition of the Geneva translation of the Bible, printed in 1578.

XCIX.

H. C.

THE stanzas annexed to these initials are derived from a small black-lettered volume of a prose work by R. Greenham, entitled "Comfort for an afflicted Conscience." The initials agree with those of xcv.

C.

CHARLES BEST.

ONE of the contributors to Davison's "Poetical Rhapsody;" beyond which nothing is known to the editor concerning him.

CI.

ANONYMOUS

WROTE "The Lamentation of a lost Sinner," included in the Old Version of Psalms.

CII.

ANTHONY FLETCHER.

THE poem annexed to this author's name is derived from a prose volume entitled "Certaine very proper and most profitable Similies, wherein sundrie, and very many most foule vices and dangerous sinnes of all sorts are so plainly laid open, and displaied in their kindes, and so pointed out with the finger of God, in his sacred and holy Scriptures, to signifie his wrath and indignation belonging vnto them, that the Christian reader being seasoned with the Spirit of grace, and hauing God before his eies, will be very fearful, euen in loue that he beareth to God, to pollute and to defile his hart, his mind, his mouth or hands, with any such forbidden things. And also manie very notable vertues, with their due commendations, so liuely and truly expressed, according to the holy word, that the godly reader, being of a Christian inclination, will be mightily inflamed with a loue vnto them. Collected by Anthonie Fletcher, minister of the word of God, in vnfained loue in the Lord Jesu, to do the best, and all that he can, to pleasure and to profite all those that desire to know the Lord's waies, and to walke in the same." This work was published in 1595.

CIII.
ROBERT HOLLAND.

ROBERT HOLLAND, "Master of Arts, and Minister of the church of Prendergast," wrote "The holie Historie of our Lord and Saviour Jesus Christ's natiuitie, life, acts, miracles, death, passion, resurrection, and ascension." This work, from which the extract is derived, was first published in 1594. It was dedicated "To the Right Worshipfull Mistress Anne Phillips, of Picton."

CIV.
H. C.

H. C. wrote "The Forrest of Fancy. Wherein is conteined very pretty apothegmes and pleasant histories both in meeter and prose," etc. This was published in 1579, and is chiefly of a secular character. Who H. C. was, is not known. Warton considers the initials as appertaining to Henry Constable; but, as Sir Egerton Brydges observes, this perhaps proceeded from the difficulty of finding another coeval claimant, as there is nothing in the style which assimilates it to the poetical productions which that author published about fifteen years afterwards.

CV.
THOMAS STERNHOLD.

STERNHOLD was groom of the robes to Henry the Eighth: an office which he retained in the court of Edward the Sixth. Braithwait says that he obtained his situation by his poetical talents; and he appears, indeed, to have had a reputation about the court not only for his poetry, but also for his piety. As is well known, Sternhold was one of the principal contributors to the Old Version of the Psalms of David. It is generally believed that he composed fifty-

WRITERS IN THIS SELECTION. xlvii

one; but this is an error. Sternhold died in 1549, in which year thirty-seven, and not fifty-one, were first published by Day under the title of "Psalmes of Dauid, drawen into English Metre by Thomas Sternholde." In 1551, another edition was published, with seven added from the pen of John Hopkins; and seven more were added in 1556 by William Whittingham, then an exile at Geneva. The remaining Psalms were versified by different individuals, and they were first printed all together at the end of the Book of Common Prayer, in 1562, under the title of "The whole Book of Psalmes, collected into English Metre, by T. Sternhold, J. Hopkins, and others. Set forth and allowed to be sung in all Churches before and after Morning and Evening Prayer, and also before and after Sermons." In the early editions of "The whole Book of Psalmes" Sternhold's initials are affixed to the first and twenty-second inclusive, and to the 25th, 26th, 28th, 32d, 34th, 41st, 43rd, 44th, 63rd, 68th, 73rd, 103rd, 120th, 122rd, and 128th: In the whole thirty-seven, the number published.

CVI.

W. P.

The fragment annexed to these initials is derived from scraps (preserved in some volumes of ballads in the British Museum) of a work entitled "Medivs: Psalmes in fourer parts which may be song to all musicall instrumentes, set forth for the encrease of vertue and abolishying of other vayne and triflying ballads. Imprinted at London by John Day, 1563." The other two or three fragments preserved are from the Old Version of Psalms, except a prayer in prose. The whole is set to music.

CVII.
JOHN HOPKINS.

NEARLY all that is known of Hopkins, beyond the fact of his being the principal contributor to the Old Version of Psalms, and the occurrence of his name subscribed to some Latin stanzas prefixed to Foxe's Martyrology, is, that he was a clergyman and schoolmaster of Suffolk, and "perhaps a graduate at Oxford," about the year 1544. Although Hopkins at first only published seven of the Psalms, and those anonymously; yet he subsequently translated fifty-eight, as indicated by his initials prefixed. Hopkins, moreover, was the ostensible editor of the collected Psalms of the Old Version, when first published in 1562.

CVIII.
THOMAS NORTON.

NORTON was born in Bedfordshire, and became a barrister-at-law, and a poet of considerable reputation among his contemporaries. Next to Hopkins he was the largest contributor towards completing the Old Version: but some few now ascribed to him were written by John Mardley.

CIX.
WILLIAM WHITTINGHAM.

THIS learned puritanical divine was educated at Oxford, after which he went abroad, and studied in some of the German universities. Subsequently he became minister of an English congregation at Geneva; but after the accession of Queen Elizabeth he returned to England, and was appointed Dean of Durham. While at Geneva, he took an active part in the translation of that version of the Scriptures known as the Geneva Bible; and also rendered those Psalms into metre which are distinguished in the Old Version by his initials, and some others, which are only to be found in the earliest editions.

CX.

WILLIAM KETHE.

LITTLE is known of Kethe beyond the fact that he was one of those who left England to avoid persecution during the reign of Queen Mary, and that he resided at Geneva, where he composed those Psalms in the Old Version to which his initials are affixed. Warton and Strype call him a native of Scotland: he appears however to have been an Englishman. Kethe likewise contributed to the Scottish Version; arising, apparently, from the fact, that Hopkins rejected many of his translations, as he did many others.

CXI.

ROBERT WISDOM.

ROBERT WISDOM was a clergyman of the Church of England and archdeacon of Ely. He appears to have been not only a champion of the Reformation, but a firm vindicator of the Book of Common Prayer against the puritans. Like many other clergymen, Wisdom took refuge at Geneva during the reign of Queen Mary. Strype says, that "besides other books, Wisdom penned a very godly and fruitful exposition upon certain Psalms of David; of which he translated some into English metre: there is one of them, and I think no more, still remaining in our ordinary singing Psalms—namely, the hundred twenty-fifth." The initials of Wisdom are affixed in the early editions of the Old Version to this Psalm only; but there is a hymn of his preserved at the end of the singing Psalms in our old Bibles and Psalters, which will be found in these pages.

CXII.
JOHN PULLAIN.

JOHN PULLAIN was born in Yorkshire, and admitted in 1547, when about thirty years of age, senior student of Christ Church, Oxford. He preached the doctrines of the reformation privately at Saint Michael's, Cornhill, in 1556, but afterwards became an exile. On his return, after Elizabeth had ascended the throne, he was made archdeacon of Colchester: he died in 1565. Pullain contributed the 148th and 149th Psalms to the earlier editions of the Old Version; but neither of these has been retained. Bliss intimates that none of his poetical productions were extant; but the 149th Psalm is still preserved, and is given in these pages.

CXIII.
JOHN MARDLEY.

IN the early edition of the Old Version of Psalms from which we transcribe, the 118th, 131st, 132d, 135th, and 145th, have the initial M. affixed. In the later editions these are all ascribed to Norton; but the initial rather appears to indicate John Mardley. In a curious article on Sternhold's Psalms, Sir Egerton Brydges makes these remarks:—"M.; unnoticed by Ritson: it might be John Mardley, who 'turned twenty-four Psalms into English odes, and many religious songs:' supposing the first supplied number (Psalm) 132, from the last might be selected 'the Humble Sute of a Sinner,' and 'the Lamentation of a Sinner.'" The initial M. seems to have been exchanged for that of N. by degrees; for in an edition published forty years later than that from which our specimen is derived, M. is affixed only to two Psalms, the 131st and 132d.

CXIV.
ANONYMOUS.

One of the contributors to the Old Version of Psalms.

CXV.
T. B.

The hymns to which these initials are affixed appear in the early editions of the Old Version of the Psalms.

CXVI.
D. COX.

The paraphrase of the Lord's prayer annexed to this name also appears in the early editions of the Old Version.

CXVII.
E. G.

These initials likewise are affixed to a hymn in the same editions of the Old Version as the foregoing.

CXVIII.
ANONYMOUS.

A Contributor to Byrd's Collection, which appeared in 1587.

CXIX.
W. A.

Nothing is known of this author: the poem annexed to his name is reprinted from "Three Collections of English Poetry," presented by the duke of Northumberland to the Roxburghe Club. It is derived from his "Speciall Remedie, etc." which was printed in 1579.

CXX.

L. RAMSEY

WROTE " A short Discourse of man's fatall end, with a commendation of Syr Nicholas Bacon," which was printed as a broadside in 1578.

CXXI.

W. ELDERTON

WROTE an " Epytaphe upon Bp. Juell," which was printed as a broadside. The two epitaphs on Jewel in these volumes have never before been reprinted.

CXXII.

ROBERT BURDET

WROTE a broadside entitled " The Refuge of a Sinner," which was printed in 1565. It is supposed that he was father or grandfather of Sir Thomas, the first baronet of the family.

CXXIII.

JUD SMITH.

THIS author wrote " A Mysticall Devise, etc." or a paraphrase of a portion of the Song of Solomon; to which is added "A Coppie of the Epistle that Jeremye sent unto the Jewes which were led away prisoners by the king of Babilon, wherein he certifyeth them of the thinges which was commanded him of God;" being a paraphrase of the sixth chapter of the apocryphal book of Baruch. At the end is a paraphrase of " The Commaundements of God our Creator geuen by Moyses, Exod. xx." and " The Commaundements of Sathan put in practice dayly by the Pope." This work was printed in 1575.

CXXIV.

GREGORY SCOTT

WROTE " A briefe Treatise agaynst certayne errors of the Romish Church: very plainly, notably, and pleasantly confuting the same by Scriptures and auncient writers. 1570. Perused and liscenced according to the Queene's Maiestie's Iniunction. 1574." The poem is preceded by an address from "The Printer to the Christian Reader," in six eight-line stanzas, in which he says that it was published

> "Chiefly for the symple sorte,
>   in forme most playne,
> In pleasant wyse, and order shorte,
> That they may viewe with lesser payne,
> And in their mynde the same contayne."

CXXV.

CHRISTOPHER LEVER

WROTE "Queene Elizabeth's Teares: or her resolute bearing the Christian Crosse," etc.; and a poem entitled "A Crucifixe," etc., which is chiefly descriptive of our Saviour's sufferings and crucifixion.

CXXVI.

JOHN PHILLIP.

THIS author wrote a historical poem entitled " A Frendly Larum, or faythfull warnynge to the true-harted subiectes of England: Discoueryng the actes and malicious myndes of those obstinate and rebellious Papists that hope, as they terme it, to haue their golden day." This poem, of which no mention is made by any bibliographer, was dedicated " to the moste vertuous and gratious Ladie Katherine Duches of Suffolke," and was published in 1570.

CXXVII.
THOMAS MIDDLETON.

MIDDLETON was a celebrated writer in the reign of Elizabeth. His productions are chiefly secular, but he wrote "The Wisdome of Solomon paraphrased," from which our extracts are derived. This volume was published in 1597, and was dedicated to Robert Devereux, Earl of Essex.

CXXVIII.
JOHN AWDELIE

WROTE and printed as a broadside, "An Epitaphe upon the Death of Mayster John Veron, preacher."

CXXIX.
EDWARD WOLLAY

WROTE a broadside entitled, "A Playne Pathway to Perfect Rest," which was inscribed to Rowland Hayward, lord mayor of London, date 1571.

CXXX.
WILLIAM GIBSON.

THE broadside from which the extract under this author's name is derived, is not dated; but it is mentioned by Herbert as licensed to Henry Rukham in 1569.

CXXXI.
ANTHONY NIXON.

NIXON was the author of "The Christian Navy, etc.;" a work which was published in 1602, and dedicated to "John Whitgift, archbishop of Canterburie." Nixon also wrote "Elisae's Memoriall," an extract from which is printed as the concluding piece of these volumes.

CXXXII.
ABRAHAM FLEMING.

Among other works he wrote "The Diamond of Deuotion, cut and squared into six seuerall points: namely, The Footpath to Felicitie; A Guide to Godlines; The Schoole of Skill; A Swarme of Bees; A Plant of Pleasure; A Grove of Grace. Full of many fruitfull lessons availeable to the leading of a godly and reformed life." This volume, which is part prose and part poetry, was published in 1602.

CXXXIII.
EDMOND ELUIDEN.

Eluiden wrote "A Newe-yeare's Gift to the rebellious persons in the North Partes of England," which was published in 1570, and which is not mentioned by any bibliographer.

CXXXIV.
ANONYMOUS.

This author wrote "An Aunswere to the Proclamation of the Rebels in the North," which was "imprinted by William Seres," and published in 1569.

CXXXV.
THOMAS NELSON.

Nelson was the author of a work entitled, "A Short Discourse: expressing the substaunce of all the late pretended treasons against the Queen's Maiestie and estates of this realme, by sondry traytors, who were executed for the same on the 20 and 21 daies of September last past, 1586. Whereunto is adioyned A Godly Prayer for the safetie of her highnesse person, her honorable counsaile, and all other her obedient subiects."

CXXXVI.

THOMAS NEWTON.

The Epitaph from which the extract given in these pages is derived was printed as a broadside, and is not dated; but it is mentioned by Herbert as licensed to R. Johnes in 1568.

CXXXVII.

NICHOLAS BOWEMAN

Wrote an "Epitaph on Lady Mary Ramsey, etc." which was printed in 1602. One of the extracts is from that work: the other is part of an Epitaph upon Bishop Jewel, which was printed as a broadside in 1571.

I.

QUEEN ELIZABETH.

PSALM XIV.

FOOLES, that true fayth yet neuer had,
Sayth in their harts, there is no God!
Fylthy they are in their practyse,
Of them not one is godly wyse.
From heauen th' Lorde on man did loke,
To know what wayes he undertoke:
All they were vague, and went a straye,
Not one he founde in the ryght waye;
In hart and tunge haue they deceyte,
The lyppes throwe fourth a poysened bayte;
Their myndes are mad, their mouthes are wode,
And swift they be in shedynge blode:
So blynde they are, no truth they knowe,
No feare of God in them wyll growe.
How can that cruell sort be good,
Of God's dere folcke whych sucke the blood?
On hym ryghtly shall they not call;
Dyspaire wyll so their hartes appall.
At all tymes God is with the just,
Bycause they put in hym their trust.
Who shall therefor from Syon geue
That helthe whych hangeth on our b'leue?
When God shall take from hys the smart,
Then wyll Jacob rejoice in hart.
                        Prayse to God.

II.

ARCHBISHOP PARKER.

PSALME XCII.

The Argument.

Of Sabbath day the solemn feast
 Doth vs excyte by rest,
God's mighty workes that we declare:—
 Loue him for all the best.

Bonum est confiteri.

1 A JOYFULL thyng to man it is,
  The Lord to celebrate;
 To thy good name, O God. so hye,
  Due laudes to modulate:

2 To preach, and shew thy gentlenes
  In early mornyng lyght;
 Thy truth of worde to testifie
  All whole by length of nyght.

3 Upon the psalme, the decachord,
  Upon the pleasant lute,
 On sounding, good, sweete instruments,
  With shaumes, with harpe, with flute.

4 For thou hast ioyed my fearefull hart,
  O Lord, thy workes to see;
 And 1 with prayse will iust rejoyce
  These handy-workes of thee.

5 How glorious, O blessed Lord,
  Be these the factes of thine!
 Thy thoughts be depe, thy counsayles hye,
  Inscrutable, deuyne.

* * * * * *

PSALM XCII.

12 The true, elect, and ryghteous man,
　　Shall florishe lyke the palme;
　As Ceder tree in Lybanus
　　Hymselfe shall sprede wyth balme.

13 Depe planted, they, in rootes alway
　　In God's swete house to bide,
　Shall florish lyke, in both the courtes
　　Of this our God and guyde.

14 In age most sure, they shall encrease
　　Theyr fruit abundantly;
　Well likying they, and fat shall be,
　　To bear most fruitfully.

15 That is to say, they out shall preach
　　This Lord's true faithfulness,
　Who is my strength and mighty rocke;
　　Who hateth unryghteousness.

THE COLLECTE.

Almighty God, which art the contynuall ioye and perpetuall felicitye of all thy sayntes, whom thou doost inwardly water with the dew of thy heauenly grace, whereby thou makest them to floryshe like the palme tree in the celestiall courts of thy Church: we besech thee that thou would so discusse from vs the burdenous weight of sinne, that we may enioye their felowship. Through Christ etc.

PSALM CX.

The Argument.

Though David's raigne be somewhat ment,
Yet Christ is chiefe here prophecied,
Who was both kyng in regiment,
And priest in death; then after stied
To heaven to sit as priest and king,
His frendes to saue, his foes to wring,
   Wyth death the sting.

Dixit Dominus Domino.

1 THE Lord most hye, the Father, thus
 Dyd say to Christ, my Lord, his Sonne,—
 Set thou in power most glorious
 On my right hand aboue the sunne;
 Until I make thy foes euen all
 Thy low footstoole to thee to fall
    As subiectes thrall.

2 The Lord shall send from Zion place
 Of thy great power, imperiall,
 The royall rod, and princely mace,
 Whence grace shall spring originall:
 Yea, God shall say,—Thou God vprise,
 To raigne amids thyne enemies,
    In princely wyse.

3 The people, glad, in hartes delight,
 Shall offer giftes, in worship free,
 As conquest day of thy great might
 In shining shew of sanctitie:
 For why? the dew of thy swete birth,
 As morne new sprong, dropth ioyfull mirth,
    So seene on earth.

4 The Lord did sweare, and fast decreed;
 He will hys worde no tŷme repent,
 Which sayd thou art a priest indeed,
 A kyngly priest, aye permamant;

Of order namde Melchisedeck,
Whom peace and right doth ioyntly decke
         As God's elect.

5 The Lord, as shield, kepth right thy hand
To make thy raigne inuincible:
He shall subdue by sea and land
All power aduerse most forcible:
He shall great kyngs and Cæsars wound;
In day of wrath, all them confound
         By fearefull sound.

6 He iudgment true shall exercise,
As iudge among the Gentile sect;
All places he shall full surprise,
Wyth bodies dead, on earth proiect.
Abrode he shall in sunder smyte
The heds of realmes that him will spyte,
         Or scorne hys myght.

7 Though here exilde, he strayth as bond,
And shall in way but water drynke
Of homely brooke as comth to hand,
Pursued to death, and wysht to sinke:
Yet he for thys humilitie
Shall lift hys head in dignitie
         Eternally.

THE COLLECTE.

O Lord, the eternall Sonne of the Father, which wast begotten before the world was made, and art the first of all creatures, we lowly beseche thee that where, by the session of the ryhte hande of thy Father, thou subduest thy enemies, so make vs to subdue all the dominion of sinne rising against vs, to be made meete to serue thee in all godliness: who liuest and raignest one God wyth the Father, and the Holy Ghost. Amen.

III.

EDMUND SPENSER.

AN HYMNE OF HEAVENLY LOVE.

Love, lift me up upon thy golden wings
From this base world unto thy heaven's hight,
Where I may see those admirable things
Which there thou workest by thy soveraine might,
Farre above feeble reach of earthly sight,
That I thereof an heavenly hymne may sing
Unto the God of Love, high heaven's King.

Many lewd layes (ah! woe is me the more!)
In praise of that mad fit which fooles call Love,
I have in th' heate of youth made heretofore,
That in light wits did loose affection move:
But all these follies now I do reprove,
And turned have the tenor of my string,
The heavenly prayses of true Love to sing.

And ye, that wont with greedy vaine desire
To reade my fault, and, wondring at my flame,
To warme yourselves at my wide sparckling fire,
Sith now that heat is quenched, quench my blame,
And in her ashes shrowd my dying shame;
For who my passed follies now pursewes,
Beginnes his owne, and my old fault renewes.

BEFORE THIS WORLD'S GREAT FRAME, in which
    al things
Are now contained, found any being-place,
Ere flitting Time could wag his eyas wings
About that mightie bound which doth embrace
The rolling spheres, and parts their houres by space,

That High Eternall Powre, which now doth move
In all these things, mov'd in its selfe by love.

It lov'd it selfe, because it selfe was faire;
(For fair is lov'd;) and of it self begot
Like to it selfe his eldest Sonne and Heire,
Eternall, pure, and voide of sinfull blot,
The firstling of His ioy, in whom no iot
Of love's dislike or pride was to be found,
Whom He therefore with equall honour crown'd.

With Him he raign'd, before all time prescribed,
In endlesse glorie and immortall might,
Together with that Third from them derived,
Most wise, most holy, most almightie Spright!
Whose kingdome's throne no thoughts of earthly
    wight
Can comprehend, much lesse my trembling verse
With equall words can hope it to reherse.

Yet, O most blessed Spright! pure lampe of light,
Eternall spring of grace and wisedom trew,
Vouchsafe to shed into my barren spright
Some little drop of thy celestiall dew,
That may my rymes with sweet infuse embrew,
And give me words equall unto my thought,
To tell the marveiles by thy mercie wrought.

Yet being pregnant still with powrefull grace,
And full of fruitfull Love, that loves to get
Things like himselfe, and to enlarge his race,
His second brood, though not of powre so great,
Yet full of beautie, next He did beget
An infinite increase of angels bright,
All glistring glorious in their Maker's light.

To them the heaven's illimitable hight
(Not this round heaven, which we from hence be-
    hold,

Adorn'd with thousand lamps of burning light,
And with ten thousand gemmes of shyning gold,)
He gave as their inheritance to hold,
That they might serve Him in eternall blis,
And be partakers of these ioyes of His.

There they in their trinall triplicities
About Him wait, and on His will depend,
Either with nimble wings to cut the skies,
When He them on His messages doth send,
Or on His owne dread presence to attend,
Where they behold the glorie of His light,
And caroll hymnes of love both day and night.

Both day and night is unto them all one;
For He His beames doth unto them extend,
That darknesse there appeareth never none;
Ne hath their day, ne hath their blisse, an end,
But there their termelesse time in pleasure spend:
Ne ever should their happinesse decay,
Had not they dar'd their Lord to disobay.

But pride, impatient of long resting peace,
Did puffe them up with greedy bold ambition,
That they gan cast their state how to increase
Above the fortune of their first condition,
And sit in God's own seat without commission:
The brightest angel, even the child of Light,
Drew millions more against their God to fight.

Th' Almighty, seeing their so bold assay,
Kindled the flame of His consuming yre,
And with His onely breath them blew away
From heaven's hight, to which they did aspyre,
To deepest hell and lake of damned fyre;
Where they in darknesse and dread horror dwell,
Hating the happie light from which they fell.

So that next off-spring of the Maker's love,
Next to Himselfe in glorious degree,
Degendering to hate, fell from above
Through pride, (for pride and love may ill agree,)
And now of sinne to all ensample bee:
How then can sinnful flesh it selfe assure,
Sith purest angels fell to be impure?

But that Eternall Fount of love and grace,
Still flowing forth His goodnesse unto all,
Now seeing left a waste and emptie place
In His wyde pallace, through those angels' fall,
Cast to supply the same, and to enstall
A new unknowen colony therein,
Whose root from earth's base groundworke should begin.

Therefore of clay, base, vile, and next to nought,
Yet form'd by wondrous skill, and by His might
According to an heavenly patterne wrought,
Which He had fashioned in his wise foresight,
He man did make, and breath'd a living spright
Into his face, most beautifull and fayre,
Endewd with wisedome's riches, heavenly, rare.

Such He him made, that he resemble might
Himselfe, as mortall thing immortall could;
Him to be lord of every living wight
He made by love out of his owne like mould,
In whom He might His mightie selfe behould:
For Love doth love the thing belov'd to see,
That like it selfe in lovely shape may bee.

But man, forgetfull of his Maker's grace
No lesse than Angels, whom he did ensew,
Fell from the hope of promist heavenly place
Into the mouth of Death, to sinners dew,
And all his offspring into thraldome threw,

Where they for ever should in bonds remaine
Of never-dead yet ever-dying paine:

Till that great Lord of Love, which him at first
Made of meere love, and after liked well,
Seeing him lie like creature long accurst
In that deep horror of despeyred hell,
Him, wretch, in doole would let no longer dwell,
But cast out of that bondage to redeeme,
And pay the price, all were his debt extreeme.

Out of the bosome of eternall blisse,
In which He reigned with His glorious Syre,
He downe descended, like a most demisse
And abiect thrall, in fleshes fraile attyre,
That He for him might pay sinne's deadly hyre,
And him restore unto that happie state
In which he stood before his haplesse fate.

In flesh at first the guilt committed was,
Therefore in flesh it must be satisfyde;
Nor spirit, nor angel, though they man surpas,
Could make amends to God for man's misguyde,
But onely man himselfe, who selfe did slyde:
So, taking flesh of sacred virgin's wombe,
For man's deare sake He did a man become.

And that most blessed bodie, which was borne
Without all blemish or reprochfull blame,
He freely gave to be both rent and torne
Of cruell hands, who with despightfull shame
Revyling Him, that them most vile became,
At length Him nayled on a gallow-tree,
And slew the Iust by most uniust decree.

O huge and most unspeakeable impression
Of Love's deep wound, that pierst the piteous hart
Of that deare Lord with so entyre affection,

And, sharply launcing every inner part,
Dolours of death into His soule did dart,
Doing him die that never it deserved,
To free His foes, that from His heast had swerved!

What hart can feel least touch of so sore launch,
Or thought can think the depth of so deare wound?
Whose bleeding sourse their streames yet never
    staunch,
But stil do flow, and freshly still redownd,
To heale the sores of sinfull soules unsound,
And clense the guilt of that infected cryme
Which was enrooted in all fleshly slyme.

O blessed Well of Love! O Floure of Grace!
O glorious Morning-Starre! O Lampe of Light!
Most lively image of thy Father's face,
Eternal King of Glorie, Lord of Might,
Meeke Lambe of God, before all worlds behight,
How can we Thee requite for all this good?
Or what can prize that Thy most precious blood?

Yet nought Thou ask'st in lieu of all this love,
But love of us, for guerdon of thy paine:
Ay me! what can us lesse than that behove?
Had He required life for us againe,
Had it beene wrong to ask His owne with gaine?
He gave us life, He it restored lost;
Then life were least, that us so little cost.

But He our life hath left unto us free;
Free that was thrall, and blessed that was band;
Ne ought demaunds but that we loving bee,
As He Himselfe hath lov'd us afore-hand,
And bound therto with an eternall band,
Him first to love that was so dearely bought,
And next our brethren, to his image wrought.

Him first to love great right and reason is,
Who first to us our life and being gave,

And after, when we fared had amisse,
Us wretches from the second death did save;
And last, the food of life, which now we have,
Even He Himselfe, in his dear sacrament,
To feede our hungry soules, unto us lent.

Then next, to love our brethren, that were made
Of that selfe mould, and that self Maker's hand,
That we, and to the same againe shall fade,
Where they shall have like heritage of land,
However here on higher steps we stand,
Which also were with selfe-same price redeemed
That we, however of us light esteemed.

And were they not, yet since that loving Lord
Commanded us to love them for His sake,
Even for His sake, and for His sacred word,
Which in His last bequest He to us spake,
We should them love, and with their needs partake;
Knowing that, whatsoe'er to them we give,
We give to Him by whom we all doe live.

Such mercy He by His most holy reede
Unto us taught, and to approve it trew,
Ensampled it by His most righteous deede,
Shewing us mercie, (miserable crew!)
That we the like should to the wretches shew,
And love our brethren; thereby to approve
How much Himselfe that loved us we love.

Then rouze thyselfe, O Earth! out of thy soyle,
In which thou wallowest like to filthy swyne,
And doest thy mynd in durty pleasures moyle,
Unmindfull of that dearest Lord of thyne;
Lift up to Him thy heavie clouded eyne,
That thou this soveraine bountie mayst behold,
And read, through love, His mercies manifold.

Beginne from first, where he encradled was
In simple cratch; wrapt in a wad of hay

Betweene the toylfull oxe and humble asse,
And in what rags, and in how base aray,
The glory of our heavenly riches lay,
When Him the silly shepheards came to see,
Whom greatest princes sought on lowest knee

From thence reade on the storie of His life,
His humble carriage, His unfaulty wayes,
His cancred foes, His fights, His toyle, His strife,
His paines, His povertie, His sharpe assayes,
Through which he past His miserable dayes,
Offending none and doing good to all,
Yet being malist both by great and small.

And look at last, how of most wretched wights
He taken was, betrayd, and false accused;
How with most scornfull taunts and fell despights
He was revyld, disgrast, and foule abused;
How scourgd, how crownd, how buffeted, how
    brused;
And lastly, how twixt robbers crucifyde
With bitter wounds through hands, through feet,
    and syde.

Then let thy flinty hart, that feeles no paine,
Empierced be with pittifull remorse,
And let thy bowels bleede in every vaine,
At sight of His most sacred heavenly corse,
So torne and mangled with malicious forse;
And let thy soule, whose sins His sorrows wrought,
Melt into teares, and grone in grieved thought.

With sence whereof, whilest so thy softened spirit
Is inly toucht, and humbled with meeke zeale
Through meditation of His endlesse merit,
Lift up thy mind to th' Author of thy weale,
And to His soveraine mercie doe appeale:
Learne Him to love that loved thee so deare,
And in thy brest His blessed image beare.

With all thy hart, with all thy soule and mind,
Thou must Him love, and His beheasts embrace:
All other loves, with which the world doth blind
Weake fancies, and stirre up affections base,
Thou must renounce and utterly displace;
And give thyselfe unto Him full and free,
That full and freely gave Himselfe to thee.

Then shalt thou feele thy spirit so possest
And ravisht with devouring great desire
Of His dear selfe, that shall thy feeble brest
Inflame with love, and set thee all on fire
With burning zeale, through every part entire,
That in no earthly thing thou shalt delight,
But in His sweet and amiable sight.

Thenceforth all world's desire will in thee dye;
And all earthe's glorie, on which men do gaze,
Seeme durt and drosse in thy pure-sighted eye,
Compar'd to that celestiall beautie's blaze,
Whose glorious beames all fleshly sense doth daze
With admiration of their passing light,
Blinding the eyes, and lumining the spright.

Then shall thy ravisht soul inspired bee
With heavenly thoughts, farre above humane skil,
And thy bright radiant eyes shall plainely see
Th' idee of His pure glorie present still
Before thy face, that all thy spirits shall fill
With sweete enragement of celestiall love,
Kindled through sight of those faire things above.

AN HYMNE OF HEAVENLY BEAUTIE.

Rapt with the rage of mine own ravisht thought,
Through contemplation of those goodly sights,
And glorious images in heaven wrought,
Whose wondrous beauty, breathing sweet delights,
Do kindle love in high conceipted sprights;
I faine to tell the things that I behold,
But feele my wits to faile, and tongue to fold.

Vouchsafe then, O Thou most Almightie Spright,
From whom all guifts of wit and knowledge flow,
To shed into my breast some sparkling light
Of Thine eternall truth, that I may shew
Some little beames to mortall eyes below
Of that immortal Beautie, there with Thee,
Which in my weake distraughted mynd I see;

That with the glorie of so goodly sight
The hearts of men, which fondly here admyre
Faire seeming shewes, and feed on vaine delight,
Transported with celestiall desyre
Of those faire formes, may lift themselves up hyer,
And learne to love, with zealous humble dewty,
Th' Eternall Fountaine of that heavenly Beauty.

Beginning then below, with th' easie vew
Of this base world, subiect to fleshly eye,
From thence to mount aloft, by order dew,
To contemplation of th' immortall sky;
Of the soare faulcon so I learne to flye,
That flags awhile her fluttering wings beneath,
Till she her selfe for stronger flight can breath.

Then looke, who list thy gazefull eyes to feed
With sight of that is faire; looke on the frame
Of this wyde universe, and therein reed

The endlesse kinds of creatures, which by name
Thou canst not count, much less their natures
    aime;
All which are made with wondrous wise respect,
And all with admirable beautie deckt.

First, th' Earth, on adamantine pillers founded
Amid the Sea, engirt with brasen bands;
Then th' Aire still flitting, but yet firmely bounded
On everie side, with pyles of flaming brands,
Never consum'd, nor quencht with mortall hands;
And, last, that mightie shining crystall wall,
Wherewith he hath encompassed this all.

By view whereof it plainly may appeare,
That still as everie thing doth upward tend,
And further is from earth, so still more cleare
And faire it growes, till to his perfect end
Of purest Beautie it at last ascend;
Ayre more then water, fire much more then ayre,
And heaven then fire, appeares more pure and fayre.

Looke thou no further, but affixe thine eye
On that bright shynie round still moving masse,
The house of Blessed God, which men call Skye,
All sow'd with glistring stars more thicke than
    grasse,
Whereof each other doth in brightnesse passe,
But those two most, which, ruling night and day,
As king and queene, the heaven's empire sway.

And tell me then, what hast thou ever seene
That to their beautie may compared bee?
Or can the sight that is most sharpe and keene
Endure their captain's flaming head to see?
How much lesse those, much higher in degree,
And so much fairer, and much more than these,
As these are fairer then the land and seas?

For farre above these heavens, which here we see,
Be others farre exceeding these in light:
Not bounded, not corrupt, as these same bee,
But infinite in largenesse and in hight,
Unmoving, uncorrupt, and spotlesse bright,
That need no sunne t' illuminate their spheres,
But their owne native light farre passing theirs.

And as these heavens still by degrees arize,
Until they come to their first Mover's bound,
That in his mightie compasse doth comprize
And carrie all the rest with him around;
So those likewise doe by degrees redound
And rise more faire, till they at last arive
To the most faire, whereto they all do strive.

Faire is the heaven where happy soules have place
In full enioyment of felicitie,
Whence they doe still behold the glorious face
Of the Divine Eternall Maiestie:
More faire is that, where those Idees on hie
Enraunged be, which Plato so admyred,
And pure Intelligences from God inspyred.

Yet fairer is that heaven, in which do raine
The soveraigne Powres, and mightie Potentates,
Which in their high protections doe containe
All mortall princes and imperiall states;
And fayrer yet, where as the royall Seates
And heavenly Dominations are set,
From whom all earthly governance is fet.

Yet farre more faire be those bright Cherubins,
Which all with golden wings are overdight,
And those eternall burning Seraphins,
Which from their faces dart out fierie light:
Yet fairer then they both, and much more bright,

Be th' Angels and Archangels, which attend
On God's owne person without rest or end.

These thus in faire each other farre excelling,
As to the Highest they approach more near,
Yet is that Highest farre beyond all telling
Fairer then all the rest which there appeare,
Though all their beauties ioyned together were:
How then can mortall tongue hope to expresse
The image of such endlesse perfectnesse?

Cease then, my tongue! and lend unto my mynd
Leave to bethinke how great that Beautie is,
Whose utmost parts so beautifull I fynd;
How much more those essentiall parts of His,
His truth, His love, His wisdome, and His blis,
His grace, His doome, His mercy, and His might,
By which He lends us of Himselfe a sight!

Those unto all He daily doth display,
And shew himselfe in th' image of His grace,
As in a looking-glasse, through which He may
Be seene of all His creatures vile and base,
That are unable else to see His face,
His glorious face! which glistereth else so bright,
That th' angels selves cannot endure His sight.

But we, fraile wights! whose sight cannot sustaine
The sun's bright beames when he on us doth shyne,
But that their points rebutted backe againe
Are duld, how can we see with feeble eyne
The glorie of that Maiestie Divine,
In sight of whom both sun and moone are darke,
Compared to His least resplendent sparke?

The meanes therefore, which unto us is lent
Him to behold, is on His workes to looke,
Which He hath made in beauty excellent,

And in the same, as in a brasen booke,
To read enregistred in every nooke
His goodnesse, which His Beautie doth declare;
For all thats good is beautifull and faire.

Thence gathering plumes of perfect speculation,
To impe the wings of thy high flying mynd,
Mount up aloft through heavenly contemplation
From this darke world, whose damps the soule
    do blynd;
And, like the native brood of eagles kynd,
On that bright Sunne of Glorie fixe thine eyes,
Clear'd from grosse mists of fraile infirmities.

Humbled with feare and awfull reverence,
Before the footestoole of His Maiestie
Throwe thy selfe downe, with trembling innocence,
Ne dare looke up with córruptible eye
On the dred face of that great Deity,
For feare, lest if He chaunce to look on thee,
Thou turne to nought, and quite confounded be.

But lowly fall before His mercie seate,
Close covered with the Lambes integrity
From the iust wrath of His avengefull threate,
That sits upon the righteous throne on hy:
His throne is built upon Eternity,
More firme and durable then steele or brasse,
Or the hard diamond, which them both doth passe.

His scepter is the rod of Righteousnesse,
With which He bruseth all His foes to dust,
And the great Dragon strongly doth represse
Under the rigour of His iudgment iust:
His seate is Truth, to which the faithfull trust,
From whence proceed her beames so pure and
    bright,
That all about Him sheddeth glorious light:

Light, farre exceeding that bright blazing sparke
Which darted is from Titan's flaming head,
That with his beames enlumineth the darke
And dampish air, wherby al things are red;
Whose nature yet so much is marvelled
Of mortall wits, that it doth much amaze
The greatest wisards which thereon do gaze.

But that immortall light, which there doth shine,
Is many thousand times more bright, more cleare,
More excellent, more glorious, more divine,
Through which to God all mortall actions here,
And even the thoughts of men, do plaine appeare;
For from th' Eternall Truth it doth proceed,
Through heavenly vertue which her beames doe
    breed.

With the great glorie of that wondrous light
His throne is all encompassed around,
And hid in His owne brightnesse from the sight
Of all that looke thereon with eyes unsound;
And underneath His feet are to be found
Thunder, and lightning, and tempestuous fyre,
The instruments of His avenging yre.

There in His bosome Sapience doth sit,
The soveraine dearling of the Deity,
Clad like a queene in royall robes, most fit
For so great powre and peerelesse majesty,
And all with gemmes and iewels gorgeously
Adornd, that brighter then the starres appeare,
And make her native brightnes seem more
    cleare.

And on her head a crown of purest gold
Is set, in signe of highest soverainty;
And in her hand a scepter she doth hold,

With which she rules the house of God on hy,
And menageth the ever moving sky,
And in the same these lower creatures all
Subiected to her powre imperiall.

Both heaven and earth obey unto her will,
And all the creatures which they both containe;
For of her fulnesse which the world doth fill
They all partake, and do in state remaine
As their great Maker did at first ordaine,
Through observation of her high beheast,
By which they first were made, and still increast.

The fairnesse of her face no tongue can tell;
For she the daughters of all wemen's race,
And angels eke, in beautie doth excell,
Sparkled on her from God's owne glorious face,
And more increast by her owne goodly grace,
That it doth farre exceed all humane thought,
Ne can on earth compared be to ought.

Ne could that painter (had he lived yet),
Which pictured Venus with so curious quill,
That all posteritie admyred it,
Have pourtray'd this, for all his maistring skill;
Ne she her selfe, had she remained still,
And were as faire as fabling wits do fayne,
Could once come neare this Beauty soverayne.

But had those wits, the wonders of their dayes,
Or that sweete Teian poet, which did spend
His plenteous veine in setting forth her praise,
Seen but a glimse of this which I pretend,
How wondrously would he her face commend,
Above that idole of his fayning thought,
That all the world should with his rimes be fraught!

How then dare I, the novice of his art,
Presume to picture so divine a wight,

Or hope t' expresse her least perfection's part,
Whose beautie filles the heavens with her light,
And darkes the earth with shadow of her sight?
Ah, gentle Muse! thou art too weake and faint
The pourtraict of so heavenly hew to paint.

Let angels, which her goodly face behold
And see at will, her soveraigne praises sing,
And those most sacred mysteries unfold
Of that faire love of mightie Heaven's King:
Enough is me t' admyre so heavenly thing,
And being thus with her huge love possest,
In th' only wonder of her selfe to rest.

But whoso may, thrise happie man him hold,
Of all on earth whom God so much doth grace,
And lets his owne Beloved to behold:
For in the view of her celestiall face
All ioy, all blisse, all happinesse, have place;
Ne ought on earth can want unto the wight,
Who of her selfe can win the wishfull sight.

For she, out of her secret threasury,
Plentie of riches forth on him will powre,
Even heavenly riches, which there hidden ly
Within the closet of her chastest bowre,
Th' eternall portion of her precious dowre,
Which Mighty God hath given to her free,
And to all those which thereof worthy bee.

None thereof worthy be, but those whom shee
Vouchsafeth to her presence to receave,
And letteth them her lovely face to see;
Whereof such wondrous pleasures they conceave,
And sweete contentment, that it doth bereave
Their soul of sense, through infinite delight,
And them transport from flesh into the spright:

In which they see such admirable things,
As carries them into an extasy,
And heare such heavenly notes and carolings
Of God's high praise, that filles the brasen sky;
And feele such ioy and pleasure inwardly,
That maketh them all worldly cares forget,
And onely thinke on that before them set.

Ne from thenceforth doth any fleshly sense,
Or idle thought of earthly things, remaine;
But all that earst seemd sweet seemes now offense,
And all that pleased earst now seemes to paine:
Their ioy, their comfort, their desire, their gaine,
Is fixed all on that which now they see;
All other sights but fayned shadowes bee.

And that faire lampe, which useth to enflame
The hearts of men with selfe-consuming fyre,
Thenceforth seemes fowle, and full of sinfull blame;
And all that pompe to which proud minds aspyre
By name of Honor, and so much desyre,
Seemes to them basenesse, and all riches drosse,
And all mirth sadnesse, and all lucre losse.

So full their eyes are of that glorious sight,
And senses fraught with such satietie,
That in nought else on earth they can delight,
But in th' aspect of that felicitie,
Which they have written in theyr inward ey;
On which they feed, and in theyr fastened mynd
All happie ioy and full contentment fynd.

Ah then, my hungry Soule! which long hast fed
On idle fancies of thy foolish thought,
And, with false Beautie's flattring bait misled
Hast after vaine deceiptfull shadowes sought,
Which all are fled, and now have left thee nought

But late repentance through thy follie's prief;
Ah! ceasse to gaze on matter of thy grief:

And looke at last up to that Soveraigne Light,
From whose pure beams al perfect Beauty springs,
That kindleth love in every godly spright,
Even the love of God; which loathing brings
Of this vile world and these gay-seeming things;
With whose sweet pleasures being so possest,
Thy straying thoughts henceforth for ever rest.

THE RUINES OF TIME.

I.

I saw an Image, all of massie gold,
Placed on high upon an altare faire,
That all which did the same from farre beholde
Might worship it, and fall on lowest staire.
Not that great Idoll might with this compaire,
To which th' Assyrian Tyrant would have made
The holie brethren falslie to have praid.
But th' altare, on the which this Image staid,
Was (O great pitie!) built of brickle clay,
That shortly the foundation decaid,
With showres of heaven and tempests worne away;
Then downe it fell, and low in ashes lay,
Scorned of everie one, which by it went;
That I, it seeing, dearelie did lament.

II.

Next unto this a statelie Towre appeared,
Built of all richest stone that might bee found,
And nigh unto the heavens in height upreared,
But placed on a spot of sandie ground:
Not that great Towre, which is so much renownd

For tongues' confusion in Holie Writ,
King Ninus' worke, might be compar'd to it.
But O vaine labours of terrestriall wit,
That buildes so stronglie on so frayle a soyle,
As with each storme does fall away, and flit.
And gives the fruite of all your travailes' toyle,
To be the pray of Tyme, and Fortune's spoyle!
I saw this Towre fall sodainelie to dust,
That nigh with griefe thereof my heart was brust.

III.

Then did I see a pleasant Paradize,
Full of sweete flowres and daintiest delights,
Such as on earth man could not more devize,
With pleasures choyce to feed his cheerefull
    sprights:
Not that which Merlin by his magicke slights
Made for the gentle Squire, to entertaine
His fayre Belphœbe, could this gardine staine.
But O short pleasure bought with lasting paine!
Why will hereafter anie flesh delight
In earthlie blis, and ioy in pleasures vaine,
Since that I sawe this gardine wasted quite,
That where it was scarce seemed anie sight?
That I, which once that beautie did beholde,
Could not from teares my melting eyes with-holde.

IV.

Soone after this a Giaunt came in place,
Of wondrous powre, and of exceeding stature,
That none durst vewe the horror of his face;
Yet was he milde of speach, and meeke of nature:
Not he, which in despight of his Creatour
With railing tearmes defied the Iewish hoast
Might with this mightie one in hugenes boast;
For from the one he could to th' other coast

Stretch his strong thighes, and th' ocean over-
    stride,
And reach his hand into his enemies' hoast.
But see the end of pompe and fleshlie pride!
One of his feete unwares from him did slide,
That downe hee fell into the deepe abisse,
Where drownd with him is all his earthlie blisse.

V.

Then did I see a Bridge, made all of golde,
Over the sea from one to other side,
Withouten prop or pillour it t' uphólde,
But like the coulored rainbowe arched wide:
Not that great Arche, with Traian edifide,
To be a wonder to all age ensuing,
Was matchable to this in equall vewing.
But, ah! what bootes it to see earthlie thing
In glorie or in greatnes to excell,
Sith time doth greatest things to ruine bring?
This goodlie Bridge, one foote not fastned well,
Gan faile, and all the rest downe shortlie fell:
Ne of so brave a building ought remained,
That griefe thereof my spirite greatly pained.

VI.

I saw two Beares, as white as anie milke,
Lying together in a mightie cave,
Of milde aspect, and haire as soft as silke,
That salvage nature seemed not to have,
Nor after greedie spoyle of bloud to crave:
Two fairer beasts might not elswhere be found,
Although the compast world were sought around.
But what can long abide above this ground
In state of blis, or stedfast happinesse?
The cave, in which these Beares lay sleeping
    sound,

Was but of earth, and with her weightinesse
Upon them fell, and did unwares oppresse;
That for great sorrow of their sudden fate
Henceforth all world's felicitie I hate.

Much was I troubled in my heavie spright
At sight of these sad spectacles forepast,
That all my senses were bereaved quight,
And I in minde remained sore agast,
Distraught twixt feare and pitie; when at last
I heard a voyce, which loudly to me called,
That with the suddein shrill I was appalled.
Behold (said it) and by ensample see,
That all is vanitie and griefe of minde,
Ne other comfort in this world can be,
But hope of heaven, and heart to God inclinde;
For all the rest must needs be left behinde.
With that it bad me to the other side
To cast mine eye, when other sights I spide.

I.

Upon that famous River's further shore
There stood a snowie Swan of heavenly hiew,
And gentle kinde, as ever fowle afore:
A fairer one in all the goodlie criew
Of white Strimonian brood might no man view:
There he most sweetly sung the prophecie
Of his owne death in dolefull elegie.
At last, when all his mourning melodie
He ended had, that both the shores resounded,
Feeling the fit that him forewarnd to die,
With loftie flight above the earth he bounded,
And out of sight to highest heaven mounted,
Where now he is become an heavenly signe;
There now the ioy is his, here sorrow mine.

II.

Whilest thus I looked, loe! adowne the lee
I saw an Harpe stroong all with silver twyne,
And made of golde and costlie yvorie,
Swimming, that whilome seemed to have been
The Harpe, on which Dan Orpheus was seene
Wylde beasts and forrests after him to lead,
But was th' harpe of Philisides now dead.
At length out of the river it was reard
And borne above the cloudes to be divin'd,
Whilst all the way most heavenly noyse was
    heard
Of the strings, stirred with the warbling wind,
That wrought both ioy and sorrow in my mind:
So now in heaven a signe it doth appeare,
The Harpe well knowne beside the Northern
    Beare.

III.

Soone after this I saw on th' other side
A curious Coffer made of Heben wood,
That in it did most precious treasure hide,
Exceeding all this baser worldës good:
Yet through the overflowing of the flood
It almost drowned was, and done to nought,
That sight thereof much griev'd my pensive
    thought.
At length, when most in perill it was brought,
Two Angels, downe descending with swift flight,
Out of the swelling streame it lightly caught,
And twixt their blessed armes it carried quight
Above the reach of anie living sight:
So now it is transform'd into that starre,
In which all heavenly treasures locked are.

MAMMON.

At last he came unto a gloomy glade,
Cover'd with boughes and shrubs from heaven's
 light,
Where as he sitting found in secret shade
An uncouth salvage and uncivile wight,
Of griesley hew and fowle ill-favour'd sight:
His face with smoke was tand, and eies were
 bleard,
His head and beard with sout were ill bedight,
His cole-blacke hands did seem to have beene
 seard
In smythe's fire-spitting forge, and nayles like
 clawes appeard.

His yron cote, all overgrowne with rust,
Was underneath enveloped with gold.;
Whose glistring glosse, darkned with filthy dust,
Well yet appeared to have beene of old
A worke of rich entayle and curious mould,
Woven with antickes and wyld ymagery:
And in his lap a masse of coyne he told,
And turned upside downe, to feede his eye
And covetous desire with his huge threasury.

And round about him lay on every side
Great heapes of gold that never could be spent;
Of which some were rude oure, not purifide
Of Mulciber's devouring element;
Some others were new driven, and distent
Into great ingowes and to wedges square;
Some in round plates withouten moniment:
But most were stampt, and in their metal bare
The antique shapes of Kings and Kesars straung
 and rare.

THE MINISTRY OF ANGELS.

And is there care in heaven? And is there love
In heavenly spirits to these creatures bace,
That may compassion of their evils move?
There is: else much more wretched were the cace
Of men then beasts. But O! th' exceeding grace
Of Highest God, that loves his creatures so,
And all his workes with mercy doth embrace,
That blessed angels he sends to and fro,
To serve to wicked man, to serve his wicked foe!

How oft do they their silver bowers leave
To come to succour us that succour want!
How oft do they with golden pineons cleave
The flitting skyes, like flying pursuivant,
Against fowle feendes to ayd us militant!
They for us fight, they watch and dewly ward,
And their bright squadrons round about us plant;
And all for love and nothing for reward:
O, why should Hevenly God to men have such
    regard!

THE WAYS OF GOD UNSEARCHABLE.

Of things unseene how canst thou deeme
    aright—
Then answered the righteous Artegall—
Sith thou misdeem'st so much of things in sight?
What though; the sea with waves continuall
Doe eate the earth? it is no more at all:
Ne is the earth the lesse, or loseth ought:
For whatsoever from one place doth fall
Is with the tide unto another brought:
For there is nothing lost, that may be found if
    sought

THE WAYS OF GOD UNSEARCHABLE. 31

Likewise the earth is not augmented more
By all that dying unto it doe fade;
For of the earth they formed were of yore:
However gay their blossome or their blade
Doe flourish now, they into dust shall vade.
What wrong then is it, if that when they die
They turne to that whereof they first were made?
All in the powre of their great Maker lie:
All creatures must obey the voice of the Most Hie.

They live, they die, like as He doth ordaine,
Ne ever any asketh reason why.
The hils doe not the lowly dales disdaine;
The dales doe not the lofty hils envy.
He maketh kings to sit in soverainty;
He maketh subiects to their powre obay;
He pulleth downe, He setteth up on hy;
He gives to this, from that He takes away:
For all we have is His: what He list doe, He may.

Whatever thing is done, by Him is done,
Ne any may His mighty will withstand;
Ne any may his soveraine power shonne,
Ne loose that He hath bound with stedfast band:
In vaine therefore doest thou now take in hand
To call to 'count, or weigh his workes anew,
Whose counsel's depth thou canst not understand;
Sith of things subiect to thy daily vew
Thou doest not know the causes, nor their courses
    dew.

For take thy ballaunce, if thou be so wise,
And weigh the winde that under heaven doth
    blow:
Or weigh the light that in the East doth rise;
Or weigh the thought that from man's mind doth
    flow:

But if the weight of these thou canst not show,
Weigh but one word which from thy lips doth fall:
For how canst thou those greater secrets know,
That doest not know the least thing of them all?
Ill can he rule the great, that cannot reach the small.

A SONNET.

Most glorious Lord of lyfe! that, on this day,
Didst make thy triumph over death and sin;
And, having harrow'd hell, didst bring away
Captivity thence captive, us to win:
This ioyous day, deare Lord, with ioy begin;
And grant that we, for whom thou diddest dy,
Being with thy deare blood clene washt from sin,
May live for ever in felicity!
And that thy love we weighing worthily
May likewise love thee for the same againe
And for thy sake, that all lyke deare didst buy,
With love may one another entertayne!
So let us love, deare Love, lyke as we ought:
Love is the lesson which the Lord us taught.

IV.

GEORGE GASCOIGNE.

DE PROFUNDIS.

From depth of doole wherein my soule dooth dwell,
From heauie heart which harbors in my brest,
From troubled sprite whych sildome taketh rest,
From hope of heauen, from dreade of darkesome hell,
O gracious God, to thee I crie and yell:
My God, my Lorde, my louely Lorde alone,
To thee I call, to thee I make my mone,
And thou, good God, vouchsafe in gree to take
      This wofull plaint
       Wherein I faint:—
Oh, heare me then, for thy great mercies sake!

Oh, bende thine eares attentiuely to heare,
Oh, turne thine eies—behold me how I waile;
Oh, hearken, Lorde, giue eare for mine auaile;
Oh, marke in minde the burthens that I beare!
See how I sinke in sorrowes euerywhere;
Beholde and see what dolors I indure;
Giue eare and marke what plaints I put in vre:
Bende willing eare, and pitie therewithall
      My wayling voyce,
      Which hath no choyce
But euermore upon thy name to call.

If thou, good Lorde, shouldst take thy rod in hande,
If thou regard what sinnes are daylye done,
If thou take hold where wee our workes begone,

If thou decree in iudgment for to stande,
And be extreame to see our 'scuses scand,—
If thou take note of euerythinge amisse,
And wryte in rowles how fraile our nature is,
O gloryous God! O King! O Prince of power!
      What mortall wight
      May then haue light
To feele thy frowne, if thou haue list to lowre?

But thou art good, and hast of mercye store;
Thou not delyhgtst to see a sinner fall;
Thou hearknest first before wee come to call;
Thine eares are set wyde open euermore;
Before wee knocke, thou commest to the doore:
Thou art more prest to heare a sinner crie
Then he is quicke to climbe to thee on hye.
Thy mighty name bee praysed then alwaye:
      Let fayth and feare
      True witnesse beare,
Howe fast they stand which on thy mercie staye.

I looke for thee, my louelye Lord, therefore;
For thee I wayte, for thee I tarrye styll:
Mine eies doe long to gaze on thee my fyll;
For thee I watche, for thee I prie and pore:
My soule for thee attendeth euermore;
My soule dooth thyrst to take of thee a tast;
My soule desires with thee for to be plast;
And to thy worde, which can no man deceiue,—
      Myne only trust,
      My loue and lust,—
In confidence continuallye shall cleaue.

Before the breake or dawning of the daye,
Before the lyght be seene in lofty skies,
Before the sunne appeare in pleasant wyse,
Before the watche—before the watche, I saye,
Before the ward that waits therefore alway,

My soule, my sence, my secreete thought, my
    sprite,
My wyll, my wish, my ioye, and my delight,
Unto the Lord that sittes in heauen on hie,
        With hastie wing,
        From me dooth fling,
And stryueth styll unto the Lorde to flie.

O Israel, O housholde of the Lorde,
O Abraham's brats, O broode of blessed seede—
O chosen sheepe, that loue the Lord indeede—
O hungrye heartes, feede styll upon his worde,
And put your trust in him with one accorde!
For he hath mercye euermore at hande;
His fountaines flowe, his springs doe neuer stand;
And plenteouslye he loueth to redeeme
        Such sinners all
        As on him call,
And faithfully his mercies most esteeme.

He wylle redeeme our deadly, drowping state;
He wylle bring home the sheepe that goe astray;
He wylle helpe them that hope in him alwaye;
He wylle appease our discorde and debate;
He wylle soon saue, though wee repent us late.
He wylle be ours, if we continue his;
He wylle bring bale to ioye and 'perfect blis;
He wylle redeeme the flocke of his elect
        From all that is,
        Or was amisse
Since Abraham's heires did first his lawes reiect.

GOOD MORROWE.

You that haue spent the silent night
In sleepe and quiet rest,
And ioy to see the cheerefull lyght
That riseth in the East:
Now cleare your voyce, now cheere your hart,
Come helpe me now to sing:
Ech willing wight come beare a part,
To prayse the heauenly King.

And you whome care in prison keepes,
Or sickenes doth suppresse,
Or secret sorowe breakes your sleepes,
Or dolours doe distresse:
Yet beare a part in dolefull wise;
Yea, thinke it good accorde,
And exceptable sacrifice,
Ech sprite to prayse the Lorde.

The dreadfull night with darkesomnes
Had ouerspread the light,
And sluggish sleepe with drowsines
Had ouerprest our might:
A glasse wherein you may beholde
Ech storme that stops our breath,
Our bed the graue, our clothes lyke molde,
And sleepe like dreadfull death.

Yet as this deadly night did laste
But for a little space,
And heauenly daye, now night is past,
Doth shewe his pleasaunt face:
So must we hope to see God's face
At last in heauen on hie,
When we haue changde this mortall place
For Immortalitie.

And of such haps and heauenly ioyes,
As then we hope to holde,
All earthly sightes and worldly toyes
Are tokens to beholde.
The daye is like the daye of doome,
The sunne the Sonne of man,
The skyes the heauens, the earth the tombe
Wherein we rest till then.

The Rainbowe bending in the skie,
Bedeckte with sundrye hewes,
Is like the seate of God on hie,
And seemes to tell these newes:
That as thereby he promised
To drowne the world no more,
So by the bloud which Christ hath shed
He will our helth restore.

The mistie cloudes that fall somtime,
And ouercast the skyes,
Are like to troubles of our time,
Which doe but dymme our eies:
Bu as such dewes are dryed vp quite,
When Phœbus shewes his face,
So are such fansies put to flighte,
Where God dooth guide by grace.

The carion Crowe, that lothsome beast,
Which cries agaynst the rayne,
Both for hir hewe and for the rest
The Deuill resembleth playne:
And as with gunnes we kill the crowe,
For spoyling our releefe,
The Deuill so must we overthrowe
With gunshote of beleefe.

The little birdes which sing so swete
Are like the angells' voyce,

Which render God his prayses meete,
And teache vs to reioyce:
And as they more esteeme that merth
Than dread the night's annoy,
So must we deeme our dayes on erth
But hell to heauenly ioye.

Unto which ioyes for to attayne
God graunt vs all hys grace,
And send vs, after worldlie payne,
In heauen to haue a place:
Where wee maye still enioye that light,
Which neuer shall decaye:
Lord, for thy mercy lend vs might
To see that ioyfull daye.

Haud ictus sapio.

GOOD NIGHTE.

When thou hast spent the lingring daye
In pleasure and delight,
Or after toyle and wearie waye
Dost seeke to rest at nighte:
Unto thy paynes or pleasures past
Adde thys one labor yet,
Ere sleepe close vp thyne eie too fast,
Doo not thy God forget.

But searche within thy secret thought,
What deeds did thee befall;
And if thou find amisse in ought,
To God for mercie call.
Yea, though thou find nothing amisse,
Which thou canst call to mind,
Yet euermore remember this,
There is the more behind.

And thinke, how well so euer it be
That thou hast spent the daye,
It came of God, and not of thee,
So to direct thy waye.
Thus if thou trie thy dayly deedes,
And pleasure in thys payne,
Thy life shall clense thy corne from weeds,
And thine shal be the gaine.

But if thy sinfull sluggishe eye
Will venter for to winke,
Before thy wading will maye trye
How far thy soule maye sinke;
Beware and wake, for else thy bed,
Which soft and smoth is made,
May heape more harm vpon thy head,
Than blowes of enmies' blade.

Thus if this paine procure thine ease
In bed as thou doost lye,
Perhaps it shall not God displease
To sing thus soberly—
I see that sleepe is lent me here
To ease my wearie bones,
As death at laste shall eeke appeere,
To ease my greeuous grones.

* * * * * * *

The stretching armes, the yauning breath,
Which I to bedward vse,
Are patternes of the pangs of death,
When life will me refuse:
And of my bed eche sundrye part
In shaddowes doth resemble
The sundry shapes of deth, whose dart
Shal make my flesh to tremble.

My bed it selfe is like the graue,
My sheetes the winding sheete,

My cloths the mould which I must haue
To couer me most meete:
The waking cock, that early crowes
To weare the night awaye,
Puts in my minde the trumpe that blowes
Before the latter daye.

And as I ryse vp lustily,
When sluggish sleep is past,
So hope I to ryse ioyfully
To iudgment at the last.
Thus will I wake, thus will I sleepe,
Thus will I hope to ryse;
Thus will I neither waile nor weepe,
But sing in godly wyse.

My bones shall in this bed remaine,
My soule in God shall trust;
By whome I hope to ryse againe
From death and earthlie dust.

V.

BARNABY BARNES.

SONNET II.

SWEETE Saviour! from whose fivefold bleeding
    wound
  That comfortable antidote distilde,
  Which that ranck poyson hath expeld and kild,
In our old wretched father Adam found
In Paradise, when he desertlesse crown'd
  Receav'd it as th' envenomde Serpent willde;
  Insteede of lustfull eyes with arrowes fillde
Of sinful loves, which from their beames abound,
  Let those sweete blessed wounds with streams
      of grace
Aboundantly sollicite my poor spirite,
  Ravishde with love of Thee, that didst debase
Thyselfe on earth, that I might heaven inherite.
  O blessed sweet wounds! fountains of electre!
  My wounded soul's balm, and salvation's nectre.

SONNET V.

BLESSED Creatour! let thine onely Sonne,
  Sweete blossome, stocke, and root of David's line,
  The cleare, bright morning-starre, give light
      and shine
On my poore spirit; which hath new begunne
With his Love's praise, and with vain loves hath
    donne.
  To my poor Muse let him his eares incline,
  Thirsting to taste of that celestiall wine

Whose purple streame hath our salvation wonne.
  O gracious Bridegroome! and thrice-lovely
      Bride!
Which—"Come and fill who will"—for ever crie;
"Water of life to no man is denyde;
Fill still, who will,—if any man be drye."
  O heavenly voice! I thirst, I thirst, and come
  For life, with other sinners to get some.

SONNET VII.

WHITE spotlesse Lambe! whose precious sweete
    bloudshed
  The whole world's sinneful debt hath satis-
    fied,
  For sinners scorn'd, whippde, wounded, cruci-
    fied;
Beholde my sinfull soule by Sathan led
Even to the gates of hell, where will be read
  My Conscience's blacke booke; unlesse supplide
  Be to those leaves past number thy wounds
    wide,
Whose purple issue, which for sinners bled,
  Shall wash the register of my foul sin,
And thence blot out the vile memoriall:—
  Then let thy blessed Angell enter in
My temple purged, and that historiall
  Of my sinnes numberlesse in deepe seas cast;
  So shall I be new borne and sav'd at last.

SONNET VIII.

LYON of Judah! which dost judge, and fight
  With endlesse justice; whose anointed head
  Was once with wounding thornes invironed,
But now with sacred crownes, by glorious right;
Whose glorious hoast succeedes in armour white;

Before whose face so many millions fled,
  And whose imperiall name no man could read;
Illuminate my thoughts with the beames bright
  Of that white, powrefull, and celestiall Dove:
Kindle my spirit with that sacred heate
  Which me may ravish with an heavenly love;
Whilst I thy ceaselesse graces doe repeate,
  Downe pourde in full aboundance to mankind,
  Which comfort in my soul, poore wretch! I find.

SONNET X.

HEAVENLY Messias! sweete anointed King!
  Whose glorie round about the world doth reach,
  Which everie beast, plant, rocke, and river teach,
And aerie birds like angels ever sing,
And everie gale of winde in gustes doth bring,
  And everie man with reason ever preach:
  Behold, behold, that lamentable breach
Which, my distressed conscience to sting,
  False, spitefull Sathan in my soule doth make.
Oh, sweete Messias! lend some gracious oyle
  To cure that wound, even for thy mercies sake;
Least, by that breach, thy temple he dispoyle.
  Helpe, helpe,—my Conscience thither him doth leade:
  And hee will come, if Thou bruise not his head.

SONNET XIII.

DEARE David's Sonne! whom thy forefathers have
  In psalmes and prophecies unborne foretolde,—
  That hell in adamantine chaines should holde,
And thence poore sinners both inlarge and save,
Whom former blindness to damnation gave:

Mee swallowed in the gulfe of sinne behold;
 A lambe amongst wild wolves, once of thy fold,
Whom Sathan now doth for his portion crave·
 Deare Sonne of David! helpe: yet helpe with speede.
Thy wounds bleed fresh in my remembrance yet,
 Which blessed wounds did for offenders bleede:
These wounds I will not in distresse forget;
 For all cheefe hope of my salvation grounds
 In nectre of these comfortable wounds.

SONNET XIV.

O BENIGNE Father! let my sutes ascend
 And please thy gracious eares, from my soule sent,
Even as those sweete perfumes of incense went
From our forefathers' altars: who didst lend
Thy nostrils to that mirrh which they did send,
 Even as I now crave thine eares to be lent.
My soule, my soule, is wholy, wholy bent
To do thee condigne service, and amend;
 To flie for refuge to thy wounded brest,
To sucke the balme of my salvation thence;
 In sweete repose to take eternall rest,
As thy child folded in thine armes' defence:—
 But then my flesh, methought by Sathan firde,
 Said my proud sinfull soule in vain aspirde.

SONNET XXI.

SOLE hope and blessing of olde Israel's line!
 Which gave, by promise, to his blessed seede
 A land that should all blessings plentie breede,
Rivers of pleasant honnie, milke, and wine;
Whose offspring numberlesse Thou calledst *thine*;

Whome with thine angels' manna thou didst
    feede,
Being before from Pharoe's bondage freede,
When Moyses first thy statutes did resigne:
  Behold, deare God! one, in these daies of grace,
(Since by thy precious bloud thou freede mankinde
  By promise,) which a portion and a place
Amongst thy children hopeth for to finde
    In gospel's comfort: through thy bloud's
        deare prise
    Oh, let him purchase such a Paradise!

SONNET XXVIII.

FORTRESSE of hope, anchour of faithfull zeale,
  Rocke of affiance, bulwarke of sure trust,
  In whom all nations for salvation must
Put certaine confidence of their soules' weale:
Those sacred misteries, deare Lord! reveale
  Of that large volume, righteous and just.
  From mee, though blinded with this earthly
      dust,
Doe not those gracious misteries conceale:
  That I by them, as from some beamesome
      lampe,
May find the bright and true direction
  To my soule blinded, marching to that campe
Of sacred soldiours,—whose protection
    Hee that victorious on a white horse rideth
    Taketh, and evermore triumphant guideth.

SONNET XXXI.

O GLORIOUS Patrone of eternall blisse!
  Victorious Conqueror of Hell and Death!
  Oh that I had whole westerne windes of
      breath!

My voice and tongue should not be so remisse;
My notes should not be so rare and demisse:
  But everie river, forrest, hill, and heath,
  Should eccho forth his praise; and underneath
The world's foundations sound that it is His!
  Hee which did place the world's foundations;
Hee which did make the sunne, the moone, and
    starres;
  Who with his bloud redeem'd all nations,
And, willing, none from Paradise debarres:—
  Shall not all instruments and voices sounde
  His glories, which in all these things abounde?

SONNET XXXIII.

THRICE puissant generall of true Christian hoast!
  Whose voyce itselfe is dreadfull thunder-cracke,
  Whose wrath doth neither fire nor lightning
    lacke,
Whose stormie frowne makes tremble everie coast,
Chasing thy fearefull foes from post to post;
  Whose hands force can all the world's forces
    sacke,
  Who turnes his foeman's colours into blacke;
Whose murthering thunderboults for arrowes bee,
  Whose sworde victorious, trenchant, double-
    edged,
His holy Scripture is; whose foes convert
  The point to their owne brest, and have
    alledg'd
Vaine arguments, thy deare saints to subvert:
  As thou, deare God! art Judge; so give thy
    doome,
  In justice, to subvert ambitious Rome.

SONNET XLVIII.

O GLORIOUS conquest, and thrice glorious speare!
  But sev'n times thrice more glorious the Name
  By which, thrice powrefull, wee conjure the same;
Which, but repeated, doth that Dragon feare,
That olde Levyathan, whose jawes, Lord! teare:
  Roote out his tongue which doth Thy saints defame,
  And thy sweete Gospell seeke to vaile with shame.
This the chief conquest of all conquests were;
  For which archangels and all angels might,
With cherubins and seraphins, out bring
  Victorious palmes, arraid in sincere white;
For which all saints might Alleluya sing.
Then, glorious Captaine, our chiefe God and Man,
Breake thou the jawes of olde Levyathan.

SONNET LI.

BREAKE thou the jawes of olde Levyathan,
  Victorious Conqueror! breake thou the jawes,
  Which, full of blasphemie, maligne thy lawes,
Ready to curse, to lie, slaunder, and banne;
Which nothing but abhomination can;
  Who, like a rangying lyon, with his pawes
  Thy little flocke with daily dread adawes:
Antichrist's harrould, who with pride beganne
  Even into thy triumphant throane to prease,
And therefore his first comfort had forgonne:
  The bodie's ruiner and soule's disease;
Bawde to that harlot of proude Babilon,
  Which mortall man to mortall sinnes inviteth,—
  Teare out those fanges with which hee thy flock biteth.

SONNET LII.

Full of celestiall syrropes, full of sweete
　Are all thy preceptes, full of happines,
　Full of all comforte, full of blessednes,
Those salutations which our Saviour greete!
O let us then contende, since it is meete,
　To keepe those lawes with upright holinesse:
　O let us use and have in readinesse
Those sweete orations, prostrate at his feete:
　Begging, imploring, weeping, smiling, kneeling,
For succour, grace, and for our sinnes humbly;
　Repentance, mercie signes, in our heart feeling,
Repent, and praise our God,—for it is comely.
　O nothing doth a Christian more beseeme,
　Than Him to prayse that did his soule redeeme!

SONNET LXX.

Unto my spirit lend an angel's wing,
　By which it might mount to that place of rest,
　Where Paradise may mee releeve, opprest;
Lend to my tongue an angel's voice to sing
Thy praise, my comfort—and for ever bring
　My notes thereof from the bright East to West.
　Thy mercy lend unto my soule distrest,
Thy grace unto my wits:—then shall the sling
　Of righteousnesse that monster Sathan kill,
Who with dispaire my deare salvation dared;
　And, like the Philistine, stoode breathing still
Proud threats against my soule, for heaven prepared.
　At length, I like an angell shall appeare
　In spotless white, an angel's crowne to weare.

SONNET LXXVI.

As those three kings, touch'd with a sacred zeale,
  By presents rich made royal offerture,
  Our new-borne Saviour's blessing to procure,
Borne in an oxe-stall for our publique weale,
When in adoring Him they did reveale
  His Godhead, by those gifts they did assure:
  So let Faith, Hope, and Love, make overture
Of new salvation, which themselves conceale
  In this base mortall stable, sinne's foul place,
Where of eternal joyes they may present
  To my salvation, borne of thy deare grace,
Such rich propines as, from thy Gospel sent,
  By precious incense may my spirit bring,
  The tearmless praises of my God to sing.

SONNET LXXX.

A BLAST of winde, a momentarie breath,
  A watrie bubble simbolizde with ayre,
  A sunne-blown rose, but for a season fayre,
A ghostly glaunce, a skeleton of death,
A morning-dew perling the grasse beneath,
  Whose moysture sunne's appearance doth impaire;
  A lightning glimse, a muse of thought and care,
A planet's shot, a shade which followeth,
  A voice which vanisheth so soone as heard,
The thriftlesse heire of time, a rowling wave,
  A shewe no more in action than regard,
A masse of dust, world's momentarie slave,
  Is Man, in state of our olde Adam made,
  Soone borne to die, soone flourishing to fade.

SONNET LXXXIII.

Ride on in glorie, on the morning's wings,
 Thrice puissant Conqueror, in glorie ride;
 That heaven, as horse, couragious doth bestride,
Who, whether thou disposest, succour brings.
Ride on the glorious cloudes, high King of kings!
 Thy conquering sworde girde to thy puissant side;
 Bright soldiours muster up, whose armies guide,
Raungde into quadraines and triumphant rings.
 That shamelesse strumpet of proud Babilon,
Which thine apostles killes, and prophets stoneth,
 With cuppe full of abhomination,
Which poysons millions, and no man bemoneth,
 With her false, proud, and antichristian route
 Suppresse, and put to slaughter rounde about.

SONNET LXXXXII.

Releeve my soule with thy deare mercies balmes;
 Monarch of precious mercie! succour send:
 I will indevour my vile sinnes to mend,
And to thee my soule sacrifice in psalmes.
High God! whose holy Spirit outrage calmes,
 Calme thou my sinfull spirites, which intend
 To thy great praise their faculties to lend.
On my soul's knees I lift my spirit's palmes,
 With humble penitence to purchase grace:
These eyes, this mortall bodie's skies, down power
 Tears of contrition on my blushing face.
Fruites of repentance flourish with this shower:
 My soule I feele is comforted and easde:—
 Then, Lorde! with my poore offering be well pleasde.

SONNET LXXXXVIII.

Where shall I, vexde, my sinfull head repose?
 If that in errour and conceived vice,
 Which with deceitful blandishments intice
My feeble nature, mortified with sinne;
Then Hope shall gates of my salvation close
 Against my soule, and my despaire beginne:
 If that in open sight, then open shame
The scarlet of my conscience will disclose,
 And sound the shameful trumpet of my fame:
Where shall I then my vexed soul dispose?
 If not in blind obscuritie nor light,
Then there, even there, in penitence with those
 Which weepe downe teares of comfort, to delight
 Their soule enlarged from eternall night.

HYMNE

To the glorious honour of the most blessed and indivisible Trinitie.

Sacred, deare Father of all things created!
 Whose joyfull throne of endlesse triumph stands
In glorious Heaven; whose name Earth animated
 Proclaymeth through the compasse of all landes;
 I lift these humble handes,
Upheavde with courage of a zealous harte,
 Confirmde with fortitude of constant fayth,
Assur'd in grace of some sweete mercies parte;
 Which treasures my deare hope in high heaven layth,
 Which comforte my soule hath.
And Thou, deare only Sonne of God alone!
 Thou precious immolacion of mankinde!

Who sits on right hande of thy Father's throne,
  Who fearful Sathan did in fetters binde;
    Whom Death alone did finde
To be the peerlesse champion of his foyle;
  Thou, that redeemedst from infernall payne
Our great grandfathers, and ourselves assoyle
  Of our foul sinnes; nor humbled, didst disdayne
    For mankinde to be slayne.
And lastly Thou, sweete comfortable Spirite
  Of meekenesse, holinesse, and spotlesse love!
By whose dear incense (not our vayne demerite)
  We purchase heritage in heaven above:
    Thou, that in form of Dove
    Thy sanctified Apostles didst salute;
  Spirite of Truth, which doth our comforte bring;
Without whose heavenly motions men are mute;
  By whose power in the virgine's womb did spring
    Our Comforter and King!
And Thou, deare sacred Father! of like power,
  With thy most deare Sonne, sacrifice for sinne;
And Thou, sweete Holy Ghost, who didst downe shower
  Cloven tongues of fire, true glorie for to winne;
    All which three Powers cloase in
One sacred and indivisible God!
  Vouchsafe, Oh! you perpetuall Highest Powers,
Of equal vertues, yet in number odde,
  These simple fruites of my repentant howers;
    And with your grace's showers
    The temper of my feeble wittes renewe,
    To prosper, cherish'd with celestiall dewe.

VI.

SIR PHILIP SIDNEY, AND THE COUNTESS OF PEMBROKE.

PSALME IV.

Cum invocarem.

HEARE me, O heare me, when I call,
  O God, God of my equity!
  Thou sett'st me free when I was thrall:
  Have mercy therefore still on me,
  And hearken how I pray to thee.

O men, whose fathers were but men,
  Till when will ye my honor high
  Stain with your blasphemies? till when
  Such pleasure take in vanity,
  And only háunt where lies do lye?

Yet know this to, that God did take,
  When he chose me, a godly one:
  Such one, I say, that when I make
  My crying plaintes to him alone,
  He will give good eare to my moane.

O, tremble then with awfull will;
  Sinne from all rule in you depose.
  Talk with your harts, and yet be still;
  And, when your chamber you do close,
  Your selves yet to your selves disclose.

The sacrifices sacrifie
  Of just desires on justice staid:
  Trust in that Lord that cannot ly.
  Indeed, full many folkes have said,
  From whence shall come to us such aid?

But, Lord, lift thou upon our sight
  The shining cleerenes of thy face;
Where I have found more hart's delight,
Then they whose store in harvest's space
Of grain and wine fills stoaring place.

So I in peace and peacefull blisse
  Will lay mee downe and take my rest:
For it is thou, Lord, thou it is,
By pow'r of whose own onely brest
I dwell, laid up in safest neast.

PSALME VI.

Domine, ne in furore.

Lord, lett not mee a worm by thee be shent,
  While thou art in the heate of thy displeasure;
Nor let thy rage of my due punishment
  Become the measure.

But mercy, Lord, lett mercy thine descend,
  For I am weake, and in my weaknes languish:
Lord, help, for ev'n my bones their marrow spend
  With cruel anguish.

Nay, ev'n my soule fell troubles do appall.
  Alas! how long, my God, wilt thou delay me?
Turn thee, sweete Lord, and from this ougly fall,
  My deere God, stay me.

Mercy, O mercy, Lord, for mercy sake,
  For death doth kill the wittnes of thy glory:
Can of thy praise the tongues entombed make
  A heavenly story?

Loe, I am tir'd while still I sigh and grone:
  My moistned bed proofes of my sorrow showeth:
My bed—while I with black night moorn alone—
  With my teares floweth.

Woe, like a moth, my face's beutie eates,
  And age pul'd on with paines all freshnes
    fretteth;
The while a swarm of foes with vexing feates
        My life besetteth.

Get hence, you evill, who in my ill rejoice,
  In all whose workes vainenesse is ever raigning;
For God hath heard the weeping sobbing voice
        Of my complayning.

The Lord my suite did heare, and gently heare:
  They shall be sham'd and vext, that breed my
    crying,
And turn their backs, and straight on backs
    appeare
        Their shamfull flying.

PSALME XIII.

Usque quo, Domine?

How long, O Lord, shall I forgotten be?
        What, ever?
How long wilt thou thy hidden face from me
        Dissever?

How long shall I consult with carefull sprite
        In anguish?
How long shall I with foes' triumphant might
        Thus languish?

Behold me, Lord; let to thy hearing creep
        My crying:
Nay, give me eyes and light, least that I sleep
        In dying:

Least my foe bragg, that in my ruyne he
        Prevailed;
And at my fall they joy that, troublous, me
        Assailed.

Noe! noe! I trust on thee, and joy in thy
     Greate pitty:
Still, therefore, of thy graces shall be my
     Song's ditty.

PSALME XVI.

Conserva me.

SAVE me, Lord; for why? thou art
All the hope of all my hart:
 Wittnesse thou, my soule, with me,
That to God, my God, I say,
Thou, my Lord, thou art my stay,
 Though my workes reach not to thee.

This is all the best I prove:
Good and godly men I love;
 And forsee their wretched paine,
Who to other gods doe runne:
Their blood-offerings I do shunne;
 Nay, to name their names disdaine.

God my only portion is,
And of my childes part the bliss:
 He then shall maintaine my lott.
Say then, is not my lott found
In a goodly pleasant ground?
 Have not I faire partage gott?

Ever, Lord, I will blesse thee,
Who dost ever councell me:
 Ev'n when Night with his black wing,
Sleepy Darknes, doth orecast,
In my inward raines I tast
 Of my faultes and chastening.

My eyes still my God reguard,
And he my right hand doth guard;

So can I not be opprest,
So my hart is fully gladd,
So in joy my glory cladd:
　Yea, my flesh in hope shall rest.

For I know the deadly grave
On my soule noe pow'r shall have:
　For I know thou wilt defend
Even the body of thine own
Deare beloved holy one
　From a fowle corrupting end.

Thou life's path wilt make me knowe,
In whose view doth plenty growe
　All delights that soules can crave;
And whose bodies placed stand
On thy blessed-making hand,
　They all joies like-endless have.

PSALME XIX.

Cœli enarrant.

The heav'nly frame setts foorth the fame
　Of him that only thunders;
The firmament, so strangly bent,
　Showes his hand-working wonders.

Day unto day doth it display,
　Their course doth it acknowledg:
And night to night succeeding right
　In darknes teach cleare knowledg.

There is no speach, nor language, which
　Is soe of skill bereaved,
But of the skies the teaching cries
　They have heard and conceaved.

There be no eyne, but read the line
　From soe faire booke proceeding;

Their wordes be sett in letters greate
   For ev'ry bodie's reading.

Is not he blind, that doth not find
   The tabernacle builded
There by his grace; for sunne's faire face
   In beames of beuty gilded?

Who foorth doth come, like a bridegroome
   From out his vailing places:
As gladd is hee as giantes be
   To runne their mighty races.

His race is ev'n from endes of heav'n;
   About that vault he goeth:
There be no realmes hid from his beames;
   His heate to all he throweth.

O law of his, how perfect 'tis!
   The very soule amending:
God's wittnes sure for ay doth dure,
   To simplest wisdome lending.

God's doomes be right, and cheere the sprite:
   All his commandments being
So purely wise, they give the eies
   Both light and force of seeing.

Of him the feare doth cleannes beare,
   And so endures for ever:
His judgments be self verity,
   They are unrighteous never.

Then what man would so soone seeke gold,
   Or glittring golden money?
By them is past, in sweetest tast,
   Honny or combe of honny.

By them is made thy servantes trade,
   Most circumspectly guarded:
And who doth frame to keepe the same
   Shall fully be rewarded.

Who is the man that ever can
  His faultes know and acknowledg?
O Lord, clense me from faults that be
  Most secret from all knowledg.

Thy servant keepe, lest in him creepe
  Presumptuous sinnes' offences:
Let them not have me for their slave,
  Nor raigne upon my sences.

Soe shall my sprite be still upright
  In thought and conversation :
Soe shall I bide well purifide
  From much abomination.

Soe lett wordes sprong from my weake tongue,
  And my harte's meditation,
My saving might, Lord, in thy sight
  Receave good acceptation.

PSALM XXIII.

Dominus regit me.

The Lord, the Lord my shepheard is,
  And so can never I
    Tast missery.
He rests me in greene pastures his:
  By waters still and sweete
    He guides my feete.

Hee me revives; leades me the way,
  Which righteousnesse doth take,
    For his name sake.
Yea, though I should through valleys stray
  Of deathe's dark shade, I will
    Noe whitt feare ill.

For thou, deere Lord, thou me besett'st;
  Thy rodd and thy staff be
    To comfort me:

Before me thou a table sett'st,
 Even when foes' envious eye
  Doth it espy.

Thou oil'st my head, thou fill'st my cupp;
 Nay more, thou endlesse good,
  Shalt give me food.
To thee, I say, ascended up,
 Where thou, the Lord of all,
  Dost hold thy hall.

PSALM XLVII.

Omnes gentes, plaudite.

ALL people, to Jehovah bring
 A glad applause of clapping hands:
To God a song of triumph sing,
 Who high and highlie feared stands,
Of all the earth sole-ruling king:

From whose allmightie grace it growes
 That nations by our power opprest,
On foote on humbled countries goes,
 Who Jacob's honor loved best,
An heritage for us hath chose.

There past hee by: hark, how did ring
 Harmonious aire with trumpetts' sound:
High praise our God; praise, praise our King,
 Kings of the world, your judgments sound,
With skilfull tune his praises sing.

On sacred throne, not knowing end,
 For God the King of kingdomes raignes
The folk of Abraham's God to frend:
 Hee, greatest prince, greate princes gaines;
Princes, the shields that earth defend.

PSALME LXII.
Nonne Deo.

Yet shall my soule in silence still
  On God, my help, attentive stay:
Yet he my fort, my health, my hill,
  Remove I may not, move I may.
How long then shall your fruitlesse will
  An enemy soe farr from thrall
With weake endevor strive to kill,
  You rotten hedge, you broken wall?

Forsooth, that hee no more may rise
  Advaunced oft to throne and crown,
To headlong him their thoughtes devise,
  And past reliefe to tread him down.
Their love is only love of lies:
  Their wordes and deedes dissenting soe,
When from their lippes most blessing flyes,
  Then deepest curse in hart doth grow.

Yet shall my soule in silence still
  On God, my hope, attentive stay:
Yet hee my fort, my health, my hill,
  Remove I may not, move I may.
My God doth me with glory fill,
  Not only shield me safe from harme:
To shun distresse, to conquer ill,
  To him I clime, in him I arme.

O then on God, our certaine stay,
  All people in all times rely:
Your hartes before him naked lay;
  To Adam's sonnes tis vain to fly.
Soe vain, soe false, soe fraile are they,
  Ev'n he that seemeth most of might,
With lightnesse self if him you weigh,
  Then lightnesse self will weigh more light.

In fraud and force noe trust repose:
  Such idle hopes from thought expell,
And take good heed, when riches growes,
  Let not your hart on riches dwell.
All powre is God's, his own word showes,
  Once said by him, twice heard by mee:
Yet from thee, Lord, all mercy flowes,
  And each man's work is paid by thee.

PSALM LXXII.

Deus judicium.

Teach the king's sonne, who king hym self shall be,
  Thy judgmentes, Lord, thy justice make hym learn;
To rule thy realme as justice shall decree,
  And poore men's right in judgment to discern.
      Then fearelesse peace
      With rich encrease
    The mountaynes proud shall fill:
      And justice shall
      Make plenty fall
    On ev'ry humble hill.

Make him the weake support, th' opprest relieve,
  Supply the poore, the quarrell-pickers quaile:
So ageless ages shall thee reverence give,
  Till eyes of heav'n, the sun and moone, shall faile.
      And thou againe
      Shalt blessings rayne,
    Which down shall mildly flow,
      As showres thrown
      On meades new mown
    Wherby they freshly grow.

During his rule the just shall ay be greene,
  And peacefull plenty joine with plenteous peace;
While of sad night the many-formed queene
  Decreas'd shall grow, and grown, again decrease.
      From sea to sea
      He shall survey
    All kingdoms as his own;
      And from the trace
      Of Perah's race,
    As far as land is known.

The desert-dwellers at his beck shall bend,
  His foes them suppliant at his feete shall fling:
The kinges of Tharsis homage guifts shall send;
  So Seba, Saba, ev'ry island king.
      Nay all, ev'n all
      Shall prostrate fall,
    That crownes and scepters weare;
      And all that stand
      At their command,
    That crownes and scepters beare.

For he shall heare the poore when they complaine,
  And lend them help, who helplesse are opprest:
His mercy shall the needy sort sustaine;
  His force shall free their lives that live distrest.
      From hidden sleight,
      From open might,
    Hee shall their soules redeeme:
      His tender eyes
      Shall highly prise,
    And deare their bloud esteeme.

So shall he long, so shall he happy live;
  Health shall abound, and wealth shall never want:

They gold to hym, Arabia gold shall give,
  Which scantnes deare, and dearenes maketh scant.
      They still shall pray
      That still he may
    So live, and flourish so:
      Without his praise
      No nights, no daies,
    Shall pasport have to go.

Looke how the woods, where enterlaced trees
  Spread frendly armes each other to embrace,
Joyne at the head, though distant at the knees,
  Waving with wind, and lording on the place:
      So woods of corne
      By mountaynes borne
    Shall on their shoulders wave:
      And men shall passe
      The numerous grasse;
    Such store each town shall have.

Looke how the sunne, so shall his name remayne;
  As that in light, so this in glory one:
All glories this, as that all lights, shall stayne:
  Nor that shall faile, nor this be overthrowne.
      The dwellers all
      Of earthly ball
    In hym shall hold them blest:
      As one that is
      Of perfect blisse
    A patterne to the rest.

O God who art, from whom all beings be;
  Eternall Lord, whom Jacob's stock adore,
And wondrous works are done by only thee,
  Blessed be thou, most blessed evermore.
      And lett thy name,
      Thy glorious fame,

No end of blessing know:
　Lett all this round
　Thy honor sound:
So, Lord, O be it so!

PSALME LXXVII.
Voce mea ad Dominum.

To thee my crying call,
　To thee my calling cry,
I did, O God, addresse,
　And thou didst me attend:
To nightly anguish thrall,
From thee I sought redresse;
　To thee unceassantly
　Did praying handes extend.

All comfort fled my soule;
　Yea, God to mind I call'd:
Yet calling God to mynde
　My thoughts could not appease:
Nought els but bitter dole
Could I in thincking finde:
　My sprite with paine appal'd
　Could entertaine no ease.

Whole troupes of busy cares,
　Of cares that from thee came,
Tooke up their restlesse rest
　In sleepie sleeplesse eies:
Soe lay I all opprest,
My hart in office lame;
　My tongue as lamely fares;
　No part his part supplies.

At length, with turned thought,
　Anew I fell to thinck
Upon the auncient tymes,
　Upon the yeares of old:

Yea, to my mynd was brought,
  And in my hart did sinck,
    What in my former rimes
    My self of thee had told.

Loe, then to search the truth
  I sent my thoughts abroade:
Meane while my silent hart
  Distracted thus did plaine:
Will God no more take ruth?
No further love impart?
    No longer be my God?
    Unmoved still remayne?

Are all the conduites dry
  Of his erst flowing grace?
Could rusty teeth of tyme
  To nought his promise turne?
Can mercy no more clyme
And come before his face?
    Must all compassion dy?
    Must nought but anger burne?

Then lo, my wrack I see—
  Say I, and do I know
That change lies in his hand
  Who changelesse sitts aloft?
Can I ought understand,
And yet unmindfull be,
    What wonders from hym flow?
    What workes his will hath wrought?

Nay, still thy acts I minde;
  Still of thy deedes I muse;
Still see thy glorie's light
  Within thy temple shine.
What God can any find
(For tearme them so they use)

Whose majesty, whose might,
  May strive, O God, with thine?

Thou only wonders dost;
  The wonders by thee done
All earth do wonder make:
  As when thy hand of old
From servitude unjust
Both Jacob's sonnes did take,
  And sonnes of Jacob's sonne
  Whom Jacob's sonnes had sold.

The waves thee saw; saw thee,
  And fearefull fledd the field:
The deepe, with panting brest,
  Engulphed quaking lay:
The cloudes thy fingers prest
Did rushing rivers yield;
  Thy shaftes did flaming flee
  Through fiery airy way.

Thy voice's thundring crash
  From one to other pole,
Twixt roofe of starry sphere
  And earth's then trembling flore,
While light of lightning's flash
Did pitchy cloudes encleare,
  Did round with terror role,
  And rattling horror rore.

Meane while through duskie deepe
  On sea's discovered bed,
Where none thy trace could view,
  A path by thee was wrought:
A path whereon thy crew,
As shepherds use their sheepe,
  Moses and Aron ledd,
  And to glad pastures brought.

PSALME LXXXV.
Benedixisti, Domine.

MIGHTY Lord, from this thy land
  Never was thy love estrang'd:
Jacob's servitude thy hand
  Hath, we know, to freedome chang'd.
All thy people's wicked parts
  Have byn banisht from thy sight:
  Thou on them hast cured quite
All the woundes of synnfull dartes;
  Still thy choller quenching soe,
  Heate to flame did never grow.

Now then, God, as heretofore,
  God, the God that dost us save,
Change our state; in us no more
  Lett thine anger object have.
Wilt thou thus for ever grieve?
  Wilt thou of thy wrathfull rage
  Draw the threed from age to age?
Never us againe relieve?
  Lord, yet once our hartes to joy
  Show thy grace, thy help employ.

What speake I? O lett me heare
  What he speakes: for speake hee will
Peace to whome he love doth beare,
  Lest they fall to folly still.
Ever nigh to such as stand
  In his feare, his favour is:
  How can then his glory misse
Shortly to enlight our land?
  Mercy now and truth shall meete:
  Peace with kisse shall justice greete.

Truth shall spring in ev'ry place,
  As the hearb, the earthe's attire:

Justice's long absent face
  Heav'n shall show, and earth admire.
Then Jehova on us will
  Good on good in plenty throw:
  Then shall we in gladdnes mow,
Wheras now in grief we till:
  Then before him in his way
  All goe right; not one shall stray.

PSALME XCI.
Qui habitat.

To him the Highest keepes
  In closet of his care;
Who in th' Allmightie's shadow sleepes,
  For one affirme I dare:
Jehova is my fort,
  My place of safe repaire;
My God, in whom of my support
  All hopes reposed are.

From snare the fowler laies,
  He shall thee sure unty:
The noisome blast that plaguing straies
  Untoucht shall passe thee by.
Soft hiv'd with wing and plume
  Thou in his shrowd shalt ly,
And on his truth noe lesse presume,
  Then most in shield affy.

Not mov'd with frightfull night,
  Nor arrow shott by day:
Though plague, I say, in darknesse fight,
  And wast at noontide slay.
Nay, allbe thousands here,
  Ten thousands there decay;
That ruine to approach thee nere
  Shall finde no force nor way.

But thou shalt live to see,
  And seeing to relate,
What recompences shared be
  To ev'ry godlesse mate.
When once thou mak'st the Lord
  Protector of thy state,
And with the Highest canst accord
  To dwell within his gate:

Then ill, nay, cause of ill,
  Shall farr excluded goe:
Nought thee to hurt, much lesse to kill,
  Shall nere thy lodging grow.
For angells shall attend
  By him commanded soe,
And thee in all such waies defend
  As his directions show.

To beare thee with regard
  Their hands shall both be spred;
Thy foote shall never dash too hard
  Against the stone misled.
Soe thou on lions goe,
  Soe on the aspick's head;
On lionet shall hurtlesse soe
  And on the dragon tread.

Loe, me, saith God, he loves,
  I therefore will him free:
My name with knowledge he approves,
  That shall his honor be.
He asks when paines are rife,
  And streight receiv'd doth see
Help, glory, and his fill of life,
  With endlesse health from me.

PSALME XCIII.
Dominus regnavit.

Cloth'd with state, and girt with might,
　Monarck-like Jehova raignes:
He who earthe's foundation pight,
　Pight at first, and yet sustaines:
　He whose stable throne disdaines
Motion's shock, and ages' flight:
　He who endless one remaines,
One the same in changelesse plight.

Rivers, yea, though rivers rore,
　Roring though sea-billows rise;
Vex the deepe, and breake the shore,
　Stronger art thou, Lord of skies.
　Firme and true thy promise lies
Now and still as heretofore:
　Holy worshipp never dies
In thy howse where we adore.

PSALME XCVI.
Cantate Domino.

Sing, and let the song be new,
　Unto him that never endeth:
Sing all earth, and all in you:
Sing to God and blesse his name;
　Of the help, the health he sendeth,
Day by day new ditties frame.

Make each country know his worth:
　Of his actes the wondred story
　Paint unto each people forth:
For Jehova greate alone,
　All the gods for awe and glory
Farre above doth hold his throne.

For but idolls what are they,
  Whom besides mad earth adoreth?
He the skies in frame did lay:
Grace and Honor are his guides;
  Majesty his temple storeth;
  Might in guard about him bides.

Kindreds come, Jehova give,
  O give Jehova all together
Force and fame, whereso you live:
Give his name the glory fitt;
  Take your offrings; get you thither
  Where he doth enshrined sitt.

Goe, adore him in the place
  Where his pompe is most displaied:
Earth, O goe with quaking pace;
Goe, proclaime Jehova king:
  Staylesse world shall now be staied;
  Righteous doòme his rule shall bring.

Starry roofe, and earthy floore,
  Sea, and all thy widenesse yieldeth,
Now rejoyce and leape and rore:
Leavy infants of the wood,
  Fieldes and all that on you feedeth,
  Daunce, O daunce at such a good.

For Jehòva cometh, loe!
  Loe! to raigne Jehova cometh;
Under whome you all shall goe:
He the world shall rightly guide;
  Truly, as a king becometh,
For the people's weale provide.

PSALME XCIX.
Dominus regnavit.

WHAT if nations rage and frett?
What if earth doe ruine threate?
Loe, our state Jehova guideth,
He that on the cherubs rideth.

Greate Jehova Sion holdes,
High above what earth enfolds:
Thence his sacred name with terror
Forceth truth from tongues of error.

Thron'd he sitts a king of might,
Mighty soe, as bent to right;
For how can but be maintained
Right by him who right ordained?

O then come, Jehova sing:
Sing our God, our Lord, our King;
At the footstoole sett before him
—He is holy—come, adore him.

Moses erst and Aron soe—
These did high in priesthood goe—
Samuell soe unto him crying,
Got their sutes without denying.

But from cloudy piller then
God did daigne to talk with men:
He enacting, they observing,
From his will there was no swerving.

Then our God, Jehova, thou
Unto them thy eare didst bowe:
Gratious still, and kindly harted,
Though for sinne they somewhile smarted.

O then come, Jehova sing:
Sing our God, our Lord, our King;
In his Sion mount before him
—He is holy—come, adore him.

PSALME CXIII.
Laudate, pueri.

O you that serve the Lord,
To praise his name accord;
Jehova now and ever
Commending, ending never,
Whom all this earth resoundes
From east to westerne boundes.

He monarch raignes on high:
His glory treades the sky.
Like him who can be counted,
That dwells soe highly mounted?
Yet stooping low beholds
What heav'n and earth enfolds.

From dust the needy soule,
The wretch from miry hole
He lifts: yea, kings he makes them,
Yea, kings his people takes them:
He gives the barren wife
A fruitfull mother's life.

PSALME CXVII.
Laudate Dominum.

P raise him that aye
R emaines the same:
A ll tongues display
I ehova's fame.
S ing all that share
T his earthly ball;
H is mercies are
E xpos'd to all:
L ike as the word
O nce he doth give,
R old in record,
D oth tyme outlyve.

PSALME CXXV.
Qui confidunt.

As Sion standeth, very firmly stedfast,
Never once shaking; soe on high Jehova
Who his hope buildeth, very firmly stedfast
                      Ever abideth.

As Salem braveth with her hilly bullwarkes
Roundly enforted; soe the greate Jehova
Closeth his servantes, as a hilly bullwark
                      Ever abiding.

Though tirantes' hard yoke with a heavy pressure
Wring the just shoulders, but a while it holdeth,
Lest the best minded by too hard abusing
                      Bend to abuses.

As the well-workers, soe the right beleevers,
Lord, favour further: but a vaine deceiver,
Whose wryed footing not aright directed
                      Wandreth in error;

Lord, hym abjected set among the number,
Whose doings lawlesse study bent to mischiefe
Mischief expecteth; but upon thy chosen
                      Peace be for ever.

PSALME CXXVII.
Nisi Dominus.

The house Jehova builds not
We vainly strive to build it;
The towne Jehova guards not
We vainly watch to guard it.

No use of early rising;
As uselesse is thy watching:
Not aught at all it helpes thee
To eate thy bread with anguish.

As unto weary sences
A sleepie rest unasked;
So bounty cometh uncaus'd
From him to his beloved.

Noe, not thy children hast thou
By choise, by chaunce, by nature;
They are, they are Jehova's,
Rewardes from him rewarding.

The multitude of infantes,
A good man holdes, resembleth
The multitude of arrowes,
A mighty archer holdeth.

Hys happines triumpheth,
Who beares a quiver of them:
Noe countenance of haters
Shall unto him be dreadfull.

PSALME CXXIX.
Sæpe expugnaverunt.

OFTE, and ever from my youth,
  Soe now Israël may say:
Israël may say for truth,
  Ofte and ever my decay
From my youth their force hath sought,
Yet effect it never wrought.

Unto them my back did yeeld
  Place and paine: O height of woe!
Where, as in a plowed field,
  Long and deepe did furrowes goe.
But, O just Jehova, thou
Hast their plow-ropes cutt in two!

Tell me, you that Sion hate,
  What you think shall be your end?
Terror shall your mindes amate,
  Blush and shame your faces shend:

Marke the wheate on howses' topp;
Such your harvest, such your cropp.

Wither shall you where you stand;
　Gather'd? noe: but wanting sapp,
Filling neither reaper's hand,
　Nor the binder's inbowd lapp.
Nay, who you shall reape, or bind,
Common kindnesse shall not find.

Such as travail by the way,
　Where as they their paines imploy,
Shall not once saluting say,
　"God speed friendes, God give you joy;
He in whome all blessings raignes
Blesse your selves, and blesse your paines."

PSALME CXXXI.

Domine, non est.

A LOFTY hart, a lifted eye,
Lord, thou dost know I never bare:
　Lesse have I borne in things to hygh
A medling mind or clyming care.
Looke how the wained babe doth fare,
　O did I not? yes, soe did I:
None more for quiet might compare
　Ev'n with the babe that wain'd doth lye.
Heare then and learne, O Jacob's race,
Such endlesse trust on God to place.

PSALME CXXXIII.

Ecce quam bonum.

How good, and how beseeming well
　　It is that we,
　　Who brethren be,
As brethren should in concord dwell!

Like that deere oile that Aron beares,
    Which fleeting down
    To foote from crown
Embalms his beard and robe he weares.
Or like the teares the morne doth shedd,
    Which ly on ground
    Empearled round,
On Sion or on Hermon's head.
For join'd therewith the Lord doth give
    Such grace, such blisse,
    That where it is
Men may for ever blessed live.

PSALME CXXXIV.
Ecce nunc.

You that Jehova's servants are,
Whose carefull watch, whose watchfull care
  Within his house are spent;
  Say thus with one assent,
  Jehova's name be praised!
  Then let your handes be raised
    To holiest place,
    Where holiest grace
      Doth ay
        Remaine;
      And say
        Againe,
  Jehova's name be praised!
Say last unto the company,
  Who tarrying make
  Their leave to take,
All blessings you accompany,
From him in plenty showered,
Whom Sion holds embowered,
  Who heav'n and earth of nought hath raised!

PSALME CXXXVI.

Confitemini.

O PRAISE the Lord where goodness dwells,
   For his kindnesse lasteth ever:
O praise the God all gods excells,
   For his bounty endeth never.

Praise him that is of lords the Lord,
   For his kindnesse lasteth ever:
Who only wonders doth afford,
   For his bounty endeth never.

Whose skillfull art did vault the skies,
   For his kindnesse lasteth ever:
Made earth above the waters rise,
   For his bounty endeth never.

Who did the luminaries make,
   For his kindnesse lasteth ever:
The sun, of day the charge to take,
   For his bounty endeth never.

The moone and starrs in night to raign,
   For his kindnesse lasteth ever:
Who Egypt's eldest-born hath slayn,
   For his bounty endeth never.

And brought out Israël from thence,
   For his kindnesse lasteth ever:
With mighty hand and strong defence,
   For his bounty endeth never.

Who cutt in two the russhy sea,
   For his kindnesse lasteth ever:
And made the middest Jacob's way,
   For his bounty endeth never.

Who Pharao and his army droun'd,
   For his kindnesse lasteth ever:

And led his folk through desert ground,
  For his bounty endeth never.

Greate kings in battaile overthrew,
  For his kindnesse lasteth ever:
Yea, mighty kings, most mighty slew,
  For his bounty endeth never.

Both Sehon king of Amorites,
  For his kindnesse lasteth ever:
And Ogg the king of Bashanites,
  For his bounty endeth never.

For heritage his kingdoms gave,
  For his kindnesse lasteth ever:
His Israëll to hold and have,
  For his bounty endeth never.

Who minded us dejected low,
  For his kindnesse lasteth ever:
And did us save from force of foe,
  For his bounty endeth never.

Who fills with foode each feeding thing,
  For his kindnesse lasteth ever:
Praise God, who is of heav'ns the king,
  For his bounty endeth never.

PSALME CXXXVII.

Super flumina.

NIGH seated where the river flowes,
  That watreth Babell's thanckfull plaine,
Which then our teares in pearled rowes
  Did help to water with their raine:
The thought of Sion bred such woes,
  That though our harpes we did retaine,
Yet uselesse and untouched there
On willowes only hang'd they were.

PSALM CXXXVII.

Now while our harpes were hanged soe,
　The men, whose captives then we lay,
Did on our griefs insulting goe,
　And, more to grieve us, thus did say:
"You that of musique make such shew,
　Come sing us now a Sion lay."
O no! we have nor voice, nor hand,
For such a song, in such a land.

Though farre I lye, sweete Sion hill,
　In forraine soile, exil'd from thee,
Yet let my hand forgett his skill,
　If ever thou forgotten be:
Yea, lett my tongue fast glued still
　Unto my roofe lye mute in me,
If thy neglect within me spring,
Or ought I do but Salem sing.

But thou, O Lord, will not forgett
　To quit the paines of Edom's race,
Who causelessly, yet hottly sett
　Thy holy citty to deface,
Did thus the bloody victors whet
　What time they entred first the place:
"Downe, downe with it, at any hand,
Make all flatt plaine, lett nothing stand."

And Babilon, that didst us wast,
　Thy selfe shalt one daie wasted be:
And happy he, who what thou hast
　Unto us done, shall do to thee;
Like bitterness shall make thee tast,
　Like wofull objects cause thee see:
Yea, happy who thy little ones
Shall take, and dash against the stones.

PSALME CXLIV.

Benedictus Dominus.

Prais'd bee the Lord of might,
  My rock in all allarms,
By whom my hands doe fight,
  My fingers manage armes:
My grace, my guard, my fort,
  On whom my safety staies:
To whom my hopes resort,
  By whom my realm obaies.

Lord, what is man that thou
  Should'st tender soe his fare?
What hath his child to bow
  Thy thoughts unto his care?
Whose neerest kinn is nought;
  No image of whose daies
More lively can bee thought,
  Then shade that never staies.

Lord, bend thy arched skies
  With ease to let thee down,
And make the stormes arise
  From mountane's fuming crown.
Lett follow flames from sky,
  To back their stoutest stand:
Lett fast thy arrowes fly,
  Dispersing thickest band.

Thy heav'nly helpe extend,
  And lift me from this flood:
Lett mee thy hand defend
  From hand of forraine brood;
Whose mouth no mouth at all,
  But forge of false entent,
Wherto their hand doth fall
  As aptest instrument.

PSALM CXLIV.

Then in new song to thee
 Will I exalt my voice:
Then shall, O God, with me
 My ten-string'd lute rejoyce.
Rejoyce in him, I say,
 Who royall right preserves,
And saves from sword's decay
 His David that him serves.

O Lord, thy help extend,
 And lift mee from this flood:
Lett me thy hand defend
 From hand of forrain brood;
Whose mouth no mouth at all,
 But forge of false entent,
Whereto their hand doth fall
 As aptest instrument.

Soe then our sonnes shall grow
 As plants of timely spring,
Whom soone to fairest shew
 Their happy growth doth bring.
As pillers both doe beare
 And garnish kingly hall,
Our daughters, straight and faire,
 Each howse embellish shall.

Our store shall ay bee full;
 Yea, shall such fullness finde,
Though all from thence wee pull,
 Yet more shall rest behinde:
The millions of encrease
 Shall breake the wonted fold;
Yea, such the sheepy prease,
 The streetes shall scantly hold.

Our heards shall brave the best;
 Abroad no foes alarme;

At home to breake our rest,
  No cry the voice of harme.
If blessed tearme I may,
  On whom such blessings fall;
Then blessed, blessed they
  Their God Jehova call.

PSALME CXLVIII.

Laudate Dominum.

Inhabitants of heav'nly land,
  As loving subjectes praise your king:
You that among them highest stand,
  In highest notes Jehova sing.
Sing angells all, on carefull wing,
  You that his heralds fly,
And you whom he doth soldiers bring
  In field his force to try.

O praise him, sunne, the sea of light;
  O praise him, moone, the light of sea;
You pretie starrs in robe of night,
  As spangles twinckling, do as they.
Thou spheare, within whose bosom play
  The rest that earth emball;
You waters banck'd with starry bay;
  O praise, O praise him all!

All these, I say, advaunce that name,
  That doth eternall being show:
Who bidding, into forme and frame,
  Not being yet, they all did grow:
All formed, framed, founded so,
  Till ages' uttmost date,
They place retaine, they order know,
  They keepe their first estate.

When heav'n hath prais'd, praise earth anew:
  You dragons first, her deepest guests;
Then soundlesse deepes, and what in you
  Residing low, or moves, or rests.
    You flames affrighting mortall brests;
      You cloudes that stones do cast;
    You feathery snowes from wynter's nests,
      You vapors, sunnes appast.

You boisterous windes, whose breath fulfills
  What in his word his will setts down:
Ambitious mountaines, curteous hills,
  You trees that hills and mountaines crown:
    Both you, that proud of native gown
      Stand fresh and tall to see,
    And you that have your more renown,
      By what you beare, then be.

You beasts in woodes untam'd that range,
  You that with men familier go,
You that your place by creeping change,
  Or airy streames with feathers row.
    You stately kings, you subjects low,
      You lordes and judges all:
    You others, whose distinctions shew
      How sex or age may fall.

All these, I say, advaunce that name
  More hygh then skies, more low then ground:
And since, advaunced by the same,
  You Jacob's sonnes stand cheefly bound,
    You Jacob's sonnes be cheefe to sound
      Your God Jehova's praise:
    So fitts them well on whom is found
      Such blisse he on you laies.

VII.

SIR JOHN DAVIES.

THE IMMORTALITY OF THE SOUL,

PROVED BY SEVERAL REASONS:

1st, *The Desire of Knowledge;* 2nd, *The Motion of the Soul;* 3rd, *From Contempt of Death in the righteous;* 4th, *From Fear of Death in the wicked; and* 5th, *From the General Desire of Immortality.*

HER onely end is neuer-ending blisse,
  Which is th' eternall face of God to see;
Who last of ends, and first of causes is:
  And to do this, she must eternall bee.

How senselesse then, and dead a soule hath hee,
  Which thinks his soule doth with his body dye;
Or thinks not so, but so would haue it bee,
  That he might sinne with more securitie!

For though these light and vicious persons say,
  "Our soule is but a smoke, or aiery blast,
Which during life doth in her nostrils play,
  And when we die, doth turne to wind at last:"

Although they say, "Come, let vs eat and drinke;
  Our life is but a sparke which quickly dyes:"
Though thus they say, they know not what to thinke,
  But in their minds ten thousand doubts arise.

Therefore no heretikes desire to spread
  Their light opinions, like these Epicures;
For so their staggering thoughts are comforted,
  And other men's assent their doubt assures.

THE IMMORTALITY OF THE SOUL.   87

Yet though these men against their conscience
   striue,
   There are some sparkles in their flintie breasts,
Which cannot be extinct, but still reuiue;
   That, though they would, they cannot quite be
      beasts.

But whoso makes a mirror of his mind,
   And doth with patience view himselfe therein,
His soule's eternity shall cleerly find,
   Though th' other beauties be defac't with sinne.

First, in man's minde we find an appetite
   To learne and know the truth of euerie thing,
Which is connaturall and borne with it,
   And from the Essence of the Soule doth spring.

With this desire shee hath a natiue might
   To find out euerie truth, if she had time;
Th' innumerable effectes to sort aright,
   And by degrees from cause to cause to clime.

But since our life so fast away doth slide,
   As doth a hungry eagle through the wind,
Or as a ship transported with the tide,
   Which in their passage leaue no print behind:

Of which swift litle time so much we spend,
   While some few things we through the sense
      do straine,
That our short race of life is at an end,
   Ere we the principles of skill attaine:

Or God (which to vaine ends hath nothing done)
   In vaine this appetite and pow'r hath giuen;
Or else our knowledge, which is here begon,
   Hereafter must bee perfected in heauen.

God neuer gave a pow'r to one whole kind,
   But most part of that kinde did vse the same;

Most eyes haue perfect sight, though some be
    blind;
  Most leggs can nymbly run, though some be lame.
But in this life no soule the truth can know
  So perfectly, as it hath pow'r to doe:
If then perfection be not found below,
  An higher place must make her mount thereto.

Againe, how can shee but immortall bee,
  When with the motions of both will and wit
She still aspireth to eternitie,
  And neuer rests till shee attaine to it?

Water in conduit-pipes can rise no higher
  Than the well-head from whence it first doth
    spring:
Then since to eternall God she doth aspire,
  Shee cannot be but an eternall thing.

All mouing things to other things do moue
  Of the same kind, which shewes their nature
    such:
So earth fals downe, and fire doth mount aboue,
  Till both their proper elements do touch.

And as the moysture which the thirstie earth
  Suckes from the sea to fill her emptie veines,
From out her wombe at last doth take a birth,
  And runnes a nymph along the grassie plaines:

Long doth shee stay, as loath to leaue the land,
  From whose soft side she first did issue make:
Shee tastes all places, turnes to euery hand,
  Her flowrie bankes vnwilling to forsake;

Yet Nature so her streames doth leade and carry,
  As that her course doth make no finall stay,
Till she herselfe vnto the ocean marry,
  Within whose watry bosome first she lay:

Euen so the soule, which in this earthly mold
  The Spirit of God doth secretlie infuse,
Because at first she doth the earth behould,
  And onely this materiall world she viewes;

At first our mother-earth shee holdeth dere,
  And doth embrace the world and worldly things;
Shee flyes close by the ground, and houers here,
  And mounts not vp with her celestiall wings:

Yet vnder heauen shee cannot light on ought
  That with her heauenly nature doth agree;
She cannot rest, she cannot fixe her thought,
  She cannot in this world contented bee.

For who did euer yet in honor, wealth,
  Or pleasure of the sense, contentment find?
Who euer ceasd to wish, when he had health?
  Or hauing wisedome, was not vext in mind?

Then as a bee, which among weeds doth fall,
  Which seeme sweet floures, with lustre fresh and gay,
She lights on that, and this, and tasteth all,
  But pleasd with none, doth rise and sore away:

So, when the soule finds here no true content,
  And, like Noah's doue, can no sure footing take,
She doth returne from whence she first was sent,
  And flyes to him that first her wings did make.

Wit, seeking truth, from cause to cause ascends,
  And neuer rests, till it the first attaine:
Will, seeking good, finds many middle ends,
  But neuer stayes, till it the last do gaine.

Now God the Truth, and first of Causes is;
  God is the last good end, which lasteth still;

Being Alpha and Omega nam'd for this,
   Alpha to wit, Omega to the will.

Sith then her heauenly kind shee doth bewray,
   In that to God she doth directly moue,
And on no mortall thing can make her stay,
   Shee cannot be from hence, but from aboue.

And yet this first true Cause, and last good End,
   She cannot heere so well and truly see:
For this perfection she must yet attend,
   Till to her Maker shee espoused bee.

As a King's daughter, being in person sought
   Of diuerse princes, which doe neighbour neare,
On none of them can fixe a constant thought,
   Though shee to all doe lend a gentle eare;

Yet can she loue a forraine Emperour,
   Whom of great worth and powre she heares to be,
If she be woo'd but by embassadour,
   Or but his letters, or his pictures see;

For well she knowes that when she shal be brought
   Into the kingdome where her Spouse doth raigne,
Her eyes shall see what shee conceiu'd in thought,
   Himselfe, his state, his glorie, and his traine:

So while the virgin Soule on earth doth stay,
   Shee woo'd and tempted is ten thousand wayes
By these great powers, which on the earth beare sway,
   The wisdome of the world, wealth, pleasure, praise:

With these sometime she doth her time beguile,
   These do by fits her phantasie possesse;

But she distasts them all within a while,
  And in the sweetest finds a tediousnesse:

But if vpon the world's Almightie King
  She once doe fixe her humble louing thought,
Who by his picture drawne in euery thing,
  And sacred messages, her loue hath sought;

Of him she thinks she cannot thinke too much;
  This hony tasted, still is euer sweete;
The pleasure of her rauisht thought is such,
  As almost here she with her blisse doth meete.

But when in heauen she shall his Essence see,
  This is her soueraigne good and perfect blisse;
Her longings, wishings, hopes, all finisht bee,
  Her ioyes are full, her motions rest in this:

There is she crownd with garlands of content;
  There doth shee manna eate and nectar drinke;
That presence doth such high delights present,
  As neuer tongue could speake, nor hart could thinke.

For this, the better soules do oft despise
  The bodie's death, and doe it oft desire;
For when on ground the burthened ballance lyes,
  The emptie part is lifted vp the higher.

But if the bodie's death the Soule should kill,
  Then death must needs against her nature bee;
And were it so, all soules would flie it still,
  For Nature hates and shunnes her contrarie:

For all things else, which Nature makes to bee,
  Their being to preserue are chiefly taught;
And though some things desire a chaunge to see,
  Yet neuer thing did long to turne to nought.

If then by death the Soule were quenched quite,
  She could not thus against her nature runne,

Since euery senselesse thing, by Nature's light,
   Doth preseruation seeke, destruction shunne.

Nor could the world's best spirits so much erre,
   If death tooke all, that they should all agree
Before this life their honor to preferre;
   For what is praise to things that nothing bee?

Againe, if by the bodie's prop shee stand;
   If on the bodie's life her life depend,
As Meleager's on the fatall brand,
   The bodie's good she onely would intend:

We should not find her halfe so braue and bold,
   To leade it to the warres, and to the seas,
To make it suffer watchings, hunger, cold,
   When it might feed with plentie, rest with ease.

Doubtlesse all soules haue a suruiuing thought;
   Therefore of death we thinke with quiet mind:
But if we thinke of being turn'd to nought,
   A trembling horror in our soules we find.

And as the better spirit, when she doth beare
   A scorne of death, doth shew she cannot dye;
So when the wicked Soule death's face doth feare,
   Euen then she proues her owne eternity.

For when Death's forme appeares, she feareth not
   An vtter quenching or extinguishment;
She would be glad to meete with such a lot,
   That so shee might all future ill preuent.

But she doth doubt what after may befall;
   For Nature's law accuseth her within,
And saith, Tis true that is affirm'd by all,
   That after death there is a paine for sinne.

Then she which hath bene hudwinckt from her birth,
   Doth first herselfe within Death's mirrour see;

And when her bodie doth returne to earth,
  She first takes care how she alone shal be.

Who euer sees these irreligious men
  With burthen of a sicknessse weake and faint,
But heares them talking of religion then,
  And vowing of their soules to euery saint?

When was there euer cursed atheist brought
  Vnto the gibbet, but he did adore
That blessed Power, which he had set at nought,
  Scorn'd and blasphemed all his life before?

These light vaine persons still are drunke and mad
  With surfettings and pleasures of their youth;
But at their deaths they are fresh, sober, sad;
  Then they discerne, and then they speake the truth.

If then all soules, both good and bad, do teach,
  With generall voyce, that soules can neuer dye;
'Tis not man's flatt'ring glose, but Nature's speach,
  Which, like God's oracle, can neuer lye.

Hence springs that vniuersal strong desire,
  Which all men haue, of Immortalitie:
Not some few spirits vnto this thought aspire,
  But all men's minds in this vnited bee.

Then this desire of Nature is not vaine;
  She couets not impossibilities:
Fond thoughts may fall into some idle braine,
  But one assent of all is euer wise.

From hence that generall care and studie springs,
  That launching and progression of the mind,
Which all men haue so much of future things,
  As they no ioy doe in the present find.

From this desire that maine desire proceeds,
  Which all men haue suruiuing fame to gaine,

By tombes, by bookes, by memorable deedes;
  For she that this desires doth still remaine.

Hence, lastly, springs care of posterities;
  For things their kind would euerlasting make:
Hence is it that old men doe plant young trees,
  The fruit whereof another age shall take.

If we these rules vnto ourselues apply,
  And view them by reflection of the mind,
All these true notes of immortalitie
  In our hearts' tables we shall written find.

And though some impious wits do questions moue,
  And doubt if soules immortal be, or no;
That doubt their immortalitie doth proue,
  Because they seeme immortal things to know.

For he which reasons on both parts doth bring,
  Doth some things mortal, some immortal call:
Now, if himselfe were but a mortall thing,
  He could not iudge immortall things at all.

For when we iudge, our minds wee mirrours make;
  And as those glasses which material bee,
Formes of materiall things do onely take;
  For thoughts or minds in them we cannot see;

So when wee God and angels do conceive,
  And think of truth, which is eternal too,
Then doe our minds immortal forms receive,
  Which, if they mortal were, they could not doo.

And as, if beasts conceived what reason were,
  And that conception should distinctly shew,
They should the name of reasonable beare;
  For without reason none could reason know;

So when the Soule mounts with so high a wing,
  As of eternal things she doubts can moue,
She proofes of her eternity doth bring,
  Ev'n when she strives the contrary to prove.

For ev'n the thought of immortality,
  Being an act done without the bodie's aid,
Shews that herself alone could moue and bee,
  Although the body in the graue were laid.

THE DIGNITY OF MAN.

O! WHAT is man, great Maker of mankind!
  That thou to him so great respect dost beare;
That thou adornst him with so bright a mind,
  Mak'st him a king, and euen an angels' peere?

O! what a liuelie life, what heauenly power,
  What spreading vertue, what a sparkling fire,
How great, how plentifull, how rich a dowre,
  Dost thou within this dying flesh inspire!

Thou leau'st thy print in other workes of thine,
  But thy whole image thou in man hast writ:
There cannot be a creature more diuine,
  Except, like thee, it should be infinit.

But it exceeds man's thought to thinke how high
  God hath raisd man, since God a man became:
The angels doe admire this mysterie,
  And are astonisht when they view the same.

Nor hath he giuen these blessings for a day,
  Nor made them on the bodie's life depend:
The soule, though made in time, suruiues for aye;
  And though it hath beginning, sees no end.

WORTH OF THE SOUL.

O IGNORANT poore man! what doost thou beare
    Lockt vp within the casket of thy breast?
What iewels, and what riches hast thou there?
    What heauenly treasure in so weake a chest?

Looke in thy soule, and thou shalt beauties find
    Like those which drownd Narcissus in the floud:
Honor and pleasure both are in thy mind,
    And all that in the world is counted *good*.

Thinke of her worth, and thinke that God did meane
    This worthy mind should worthy things embrace:
Blot not her beauties with thy thoughts vncleane,
    Nor her dishonor with thy passions base.

Kill not her *quick'ning power* with surfettings;
    Mar not her sense with sensualities;
Cast not her serious wit on idle things;
    Make not her free will slaue to vanities.

And when thou thinkst of her eternitie,
    Thinke not that death against her nature is:
Thinke it a birth; and when thou goest to die,
    Sing like a swan, as if thou wentst to blisse.

And thou, my Soule, which turnst thy curious eye
    To view the beames of thine owne form diuine,
Know that thou canst know nothing perfectly,
    While thou art clouded with this flesh of mine.

Take heed of ouer-weening, and compare
    Thy peacock's feet with thy gay peacock's traine:

Studie the best and highest things that are,
  But of thyselfe an humble thought retaine.

Cast downe thyselfe, and onely striue to raise
  The glorie of thy Maker's sacred Name:
Vse all thy powers that blessed power to praise,
  Which giues thee power to be, and vse the same.

THE SOUL.

THE lights of Heauen (which are the world's fair eyes)
  Looke downe into the world, the world to see;
And as they turne or wander in the skies,
  Surucigh all things that on this center bee.

And yet the lights which in my towre do shine,
  Mine eyes, which view all obiects, nigh and farre,
Looke not into this little world of mine,
  Nor see my face, wherein they fixed are.

Since Nature failes vs in no needfull thing,
  Why want I meanes mine inward selfe to see?
Which sight the knowledge of myselfe might bring,
  Which to true wisdome is the first degree.

That powre, which gaue me eyes the world to view,
  To view myselfe enfusd an inward light,
Whereby my soule, as by a mirror true,
  Of her own forme may take a perfect sight.

But as the sharpest eye discerneth nought,
  Except the sun-beames in the aire doe shine;
So the best sense with her reflecting thought
  Seekes not herselfe without some light diuine.

O Light, which mak'st the light which makes
    the day,
  Which setst the eye without, and mind within,
Lighten my spirit with one cleare heauenly ray,
  Which now to view itselfe doth first begin.

For her true forme how can my sparke discerne,
  Which, dimme by nature, art did neuer cleare,
When the great wits, of whom all skill we learne,
  Are ignorant both what shee is, and where?

One thinks the soule is aire; another, fire;
  Another, blood defus'd about the hart;
Another saith the elements conspire,
  And to her essence each doth giue a part.

Musicians thinke our souls are harmonies;
  Physicians hold that they complexions bee;
Epicures make them swarmes of atomies,
  Which do by chaunce into our bodies flee.

Some thinke one generall soule fils euery braine,
  As the bright sunne sheds light in euery starre;
And others thinke the name of soule is vaine,
  And that we onely well-mixt bodies are.

In iudgment of her substance thus they varie;
  And thus they varie in iudgment of her seate:
For some her chaire vp to the braine do carrie,
  Some thrust it downe into the stomake's heate.

Some place it in the roote of life, the hart;
  Some in the liuer, fountaine of the vaines;
Some say she is all in all, and all in part:
  Some say she is not containd, but all containes.

Thus these great clerks their little wisedome shew,
  While with their doctrines they at hazard play;
Tossing their light opinions to and fro,
  To mocke the lewd, as learnd in this as they.

For no craz'd braine could euer yet propound
  Touching the soule so vaine and fond a thought;
But some among these maisters haue been found,
  Which in their schooles the self-same thing haue taught.

God onely wise, to punish pride of wit,
  Among men's wits hath this confusion wrought;
As the proud towre, whose points the clouds did hit,
  By tongues' confusion was to ruine brought.

But Thou, which didst man's soule of nothing make,
  And when to nothing it was fallen agen,
To make it new, the forme of man didst take,
  And God with God becam'st a man with men;

Thou, that hast fashioned twise this soule of ours,
  So that she is by double title thine,
Thou onely knowest her nature and her powers;
  Her subtile forme thou onely canst define.

To iudge herselfe she must herselfe transcend;
  As greater circles comprehend the lesse:
But she wants power her owne power to extend;
  As fettred men cannot their strength expresse.

But thou, bright morning Starre, thou rising Sunne,
  Which in these later times hast brought to light
Those mysteries, that, since the world begun,
  Lay hid in darknesse and eternall night;

Thou, like the sunne, dost with indifferent ray
  Into the pallace and the cottage shine,
And shew'st the soule both to the clarke and lay
  By the cleere lampe of thy oracle diuine.

This lampe through all the regions of my braine,
  Where my soule sits, doth spread such beames of grace,
As now, methinks, I do distinguish plain
  Each subtill line of her immortall face.

The soule a substance and a spirit is,
  Which God himselfe doth in the bodie make,
Which makes the man: for euery man from this
  The nature of a man and name doth take.

And though this spirit be to the bodie knit,
  As an apt meane her powers to exercise,
Which are life, motion, sense, and will, and wit,
  Yet she suruiues, although the bodie dies.

FALSE AND TRUE KNOWLEDGE.

Why did my parents send me to the schooles,
  That I with knowledge might enrich my mind,
Since the desire to know first made men fooles,
  And did corrupt the roote of all mankind?

For when God's hand had written in the harts
  Of the first parents all the rules of good,
So that their skill enfusd did passe all arts
  That euer were, before or since the flood;

And when their reason's eye was sharpe and cleere,
  And, as an eagle can behold the sunne,
Could haue approch't th' eternall light as neere
  As the intellectual angels could haue done;

Euen then to them the spirit of lies suggests,
  That they were blind, because they saw not ill,
And breathes into their incorrupted breasts
  A curious wish, which did corrupt their will.

For that same ill they straight desir'd to know;
  Which ill, being nought but a defect of good,
In all God's works the diuell could not shew,
  While man, their lord, in his perfection stood:

So that themselues were first to do the ill,
  Ere they thereof the knowledge could attaine;
Like him that knew not poison's power to kill,
  Vntill, by tasting it, himselfe was slaine.

Euen so, by tasting of that fruite forbid,
  Where they sought *knowledge*, they did *error* find;
Ill they desir'd to know, and ill they did;
  And, to giue *Passion* eyes, made *Reason* blind:

For then their minds did first in Passion see
  Those wretched shapes of miserie and woe,
Of nakednesse, of shame, of pouertie,
  Which then their owne experience made them know.

But then grew Reason darke, that she no more
  Could the faire formes of *Good* and *Truth* discerne:
Battes they became, who eagles were before;
  And this they got by their desire to learne.

But we, their wretched offspring, what do we?
  Doe not wee still tast of the fruite forbid,
Whiles, with fond fruitlesse curiositie,
  In bookes prophane we seeke for knowledge hid?

What is this knowledge but the skie-stolne fire,
  For which the thiefe[1] still chain'd in ice doth sit,
And which the poore rude satyre[2] did admire,
  And needs would kisse, but burnt his lips with it?

---

[1] Prometheus. [2] See Æsop's Fables.

What is it but the cloud of emptie raine,
    Which when Ioue's guest[1] imbrac't, he monsters got?
Or the false pailes[2], which, oft being fild with paine,
    Receiu'd the water, but retain'd it not?

Shortly, what is it but the fierie coach,
    Which the youth[3] sought, and sought his death withall?
Or the boye's[4] wings, which, when he did approch
    The sunne's hote beames, did melt and let him fall?

And yet, alas! when all our lampes are burnd,
    Our bodies wasted, and our spirits spent;
When we haue all the learned volumes turnd,
    Which yeeld men's wits both helpe and ornament;

What can we know, or what can we discerne,
    When error chokes the windowes of the minde?
The diuers formes of things how can we learne,
    That haue bene euer from our birth-day blind?

When Reason's lampe, which, like the sunne in skie,
    Throughout man's litle world her beames did spread,
Is now become a sparkle, which doth lie
    Vnder the ashes, halfe extinct and dead;

How can we hope that through the eye and eare
    This dying sparkle, in this cloudie place,
Can recollect these beames of knowledge cleare,
    Which were enfus'd in the first minds by grace?

---

[1] Ixion.   [2] Of the Danaïdes.   [3] Phaëton.   [4] Icarus.

So might the heire, whose father hath in play
  Wasted a thousand pound of auncient rent,
By painefull earning of one grote a day,
  Hope to restore the patrimonie spent.

The wits that div'd most deepe and soar'd most hie,
  Seeking man's pow'rs, haue found his weaknes such:
Skill comes so slow, and life so fast doth flie;
  We learne so litle, and forget so much:

For this the wisest of all morall men
  Said, *he knew nought, but that he nought did know;*
And the great mocking maister mockt not then,
  When he said, *Truth was buried deepe below.*

For how may we to other things attaine,
  When none of vs his own soule vnderstands?
For which the diuell mockes our curious braine,
  When, *Know thyselfe*, his oracle commands.

For why should we the busie soule beleeue,
  When boldly she concludes of that and this,
When of herselfe she can no iudgment geue,
  Nor how, nor whence, nor where, nor what she is?

All things without, which round about we see,
  We seeke to know, and how therewith to do:
But that whereby we *reason, liue, and be*,
  Within ourselves, we strangers are thereto.

We seeke to know the mouing of each spheare,
  And the straunge cause of th' ebbs and flouds of Nile;
But of that clocke within our breasts we beare,
  The subtill motions we forget the while.

We that acquaint ourselues with euery zoane,
  And pass both tropikes, and behold both poles,

When we come home, are to ourselues vnknowne,
  And vnacquainted still with our own soules.

We studie speech, but others we perswade;
  We leech-craft learne, but others cure with it;
We interpret lawes which other men haue made,
  But reade not those which in our harts are writ.

It is because the minde is like the eye,
  Through which it gathers knowledge by degrees;
Whose rayes reflect not, but spread outwardly;
  Not seeing itselfe, when other things it sees.

No, doubtlesse: for the minde can backward cast
  Vpon herself her vnderstanding light;
But she is so corrupt, and so defac't,
  And her owne image doth herselfe affright:

As is the fable of the ladie faire,
  Which for her lust was turn'd into a cow;
When thirstie to a streame she did repaire,
  And saw herselfe transform'd, she wist not how,

At first she startles, then she stands amaz'd;
  At last with terror she from thence doth flie,
And loathes the watrie glasse wherein she gaz'd,
  And shunnes it still, though she for thirst do die.

Euen so man's soule, which did God's image beare,
  And was at first faire, good, and spotlesse pure,
Since with her sinnes her beauties blotted were,
  Doth of all sights her owne sight least endure:

For euen at first reflection she espies
  Such strange chymeras, and such monsters there,
Such toyes, such antikes, and such vanities,
  As she retires and shrinkes for shame and feare.

FALSE AND TRUE KNOWLEDGE.

And as the man loues least at home to bee,
   That hath a sluttish house, haunted with sprites;
So she, impatient her owne faults to see,
   Turnes from herselfe, and in strange things delites.

For this, few *know themselues:* for merchants broke
   View their estate with discontent and paine;
And seas are troubled, when they doe reuoke
   Their flowing waues into themselues againe.

And while the face of outward things we find
   Pleasing and faire, agreeable and sweete,
These things transport, and carrie out the mind,
   That with herselfe herselfe can neuer meete.

Yet if *Affliction* once her warres begin,
   And threat the feeble Sense with sword and fire,
The minde contracts herselfe, and shrinketh in,
   And to herselfe she gladly doth retire;

As spiders toucht seeke their web's inmost part;
   As bees in stormes vnto their hiues returne;
As bloud in danger gathers to the hart;
   As men seek towns, when foes the country burne.

If ought can teach vs ought, Affliction's lookes,
   Making vs looke vnto ourselues so neare,
Teach vs to know ourselues beyond all bookes,
   Or all the learned schooles that euer were.

This mistresse lately pluckt me by the eare,
   And many a golden lesson hath me taught;
Hath made my senses quicke, and reason cleare,
   Reformd my will, and rectifide my thought.

So do the *winds* and *thunder* cleanse the ayre;
  So working leas settle and purge the wine;
So lopt and pruned trees doe florish faire;
  So doth the fire the drossie gold refine.

Neither *Minerua*, nor the learned Muse,
  Nor rules of *art*, nor *precepts* of the wise,
Could in my braine those beames of skill enfuse,
  As but the glaunce of this dame's angrie eyes.

Shee within listes my raunging mind hath brought,
  That now beyond myselfe I will not go:
Myselfe am center of my circling thought,
  Onely myselfe I studie, learne, and know.

I know my body's of so fraile a kinde,
  As force without, feauers within can kill:
I know the heauenly nature of my minde,
  But 'tis corrupted both in wit and will.

I know my soule hath power to know all things,
  Yet is she blinde and ignorant in all:
I know I am one of Nature's litle kings,
  Yet to the least and vilest things am thrall.

I know my life's a paine, and but a span;
  I know my sense is mockt with euery thing;
And, to conclude, I know myselfe a man,
  Which is a proud, and yet a wretched thing.

VIII.

FULKE GREVILLE, LORD BROOKE.

SONNETS.

I.

When as man's life, the light of humane lust,
In soacket of his early lanthorne burnes,
That all this glory vnto ashes must,
And generations to corruption turnes;
   Then fond desires, that onely feare their end,
   Doe vainely wish for life but to amend.

But when this life is from the body fled,
To see itselfe in that eternall glasse,
Where time doth end, and thoughts accuse the dead,
Where all to come is one with all that was;
   Then liuing men aske how he left his breath,
   That while he liued never thought of death!

II.

Man, dreame no more of curious mysteries,
And what was here before the world was made;
The first man's life, the state of Paradise,
Where heauen is, or hell's eternal shade:
   For God's works are, like him, all infinite,
   And curious search but craftie sinnes delight.

The flood that did, and dreadfull fire that shall,
Drowne and burne vp the malice of the earth,
The diuers tongues and Babylon's downefall,
Are nothing to the man's renewed birth:

First, let the Law plough vp thy wicked heart,
That Christ may come, and all these types depart.

When thou hast swept the house that all is cleare ;
When thou the dust hast shaken from thy feete ;
When God's All-might doth in thy flesh appeare,
Then seas with streames aboue the skye do meete :
   For goodnesse onely doth God comprehend,
   Knowes what was first, and what shall be the end.

III.

The Manicheans did no idolls make
Without themselues, nor worship gods of wood ;
Yet idolls did in their ideas take,
And figur'd Christ as on the cross he stood :
   Thus did they when they earnestly did pray,
   Till clearer faith this idoll tooke away.

We seeme more inwardly to knowe the Sonne,
And see our owne saluation in his blood :
When this is said, we thinke the worke is done,
And with the Father hold our portion good :
   As if true life within these words were laid
   For him that in life neuer words obey'd.

If this be safe, it is a pleasant way ;
The crosse of Christ is very easily borne :
But sixe dayes' labour makes the Sabboth-day ;
The flesh is dead before grace can be borne :
   The heart must first beare witnesse with the booke,
   The earth must burne, ere we for Christ can looke.

IV.

Eternall Truth, almighty, infinite,
Onely exiled from man's fleshly heart,

Where ignorance and disobedience fight,
In hell and sinne which shall haue greatest part;
  When thy sweet mercy opens forth the light
Of grace, which giueth eyes vnto the blinde,
And with the Law euen plowest up our sprite
To faith, wherein flesh may saluation finde,
  Thou bidst vs pray; and wee doe pray to thee:
But as to power and God without vs plac'd,
Thinking a wish may weare out vanity,
Or habits be by miracles defac'd,
  One thought to God wee giue, the rest to sinne:
Quickly vnbent is all desire of good;
True words passe out, but haue no being within;
Wee pray to Christ, yet helpe to shed his blood:
  For while we say beleeve, and feele it not,
Promise amends, and yet despaire in it,
Heare Sodom iudg'd, and goe not out with Lot,
Make Law and Gospell riddles of the wit;
  Wee with the Jewes euen Christ still crucifie,
  As not yet come to our impiety.

V.

Wrapt vp, O Lord, in man's degeneration,
The glories of thy truth, thy ioyes eternall,
Reflect vpon my soule darke desolation
And vgly prospects ore the sp'rits infernall:
  Lord, I haue sinn'd, and mine iniquity
  Deserues this hell; yet, Lord, deliuer me.

Thy power and mercy neuer comprehended
Rest, liuely imag'd in my conscience wounded;
Mercy to grace, and power to feare extended,
Both infinite, and I in both confounded:
  Lord, I haue sinn'd, and mine iniquity
  Deserues this hell; yet, Lord, deliuer me.

If from this depth of sinne, this hellish graue,
And fatall absence from my Sauiour's glory,

I could implore his mercy who can saue,
And for my sinnes, not paines of sinne, be sorry;
   Lord, from this horror of iniquity,
   And hellish graue, thou wouldst deliuer me.

VI.

Downe in the depth of mine iniquity,
That vgly center of infernall spirits,
Where each sinne feeles her own deformity,
In those peculiar torments she inherits—
   Depriu'd of human graces and diuine,
   Euen there appeares this sauing God of mine.

And in this fatall mirrour of transgression,
Shewes man, as fruit of his degeneration,
The errours vgly infinite impression,
Which beares the faithlesse down to desperation—
   Depriu'd of human graces and diuine,
   Euen there appeares this sauing God of mine.

In power and birth, Almighty and Eternall,
Which on the sinne reflects strange desolation,
With glory scourging all the spirits infernall,
And vncreated hell with vnpriuation,
   Depriu'd of human graces and diuine,
   Euen there appeares this sauing God of mine.

For on this spirituall Crosse, condemned, lying,
To paines infernall by eternal doome,
I see my Sauiour for the same sinnes dying,
And from that hell I fear'd to free me come;
   Depriu'd of human graces, *not* diuine,
   Thus hath his death rais'd vp this soule of mine.

VII.

The serpent Sinne, by shewing humane lust
Visions and dreames, inticed man to doe
Follies, in which exceed his God he must,
And know more than he was created to:

A charme which made the vgly sinne seeme
    good,
And is by falne spirits onely vnderstood.

Now man no sooner from his meane creation
Trode this excesse of vncreated sinne,
But straight he chaung'd his being to priuation,
Horrour and death at this gate passing in;
    Whereby immortall life, made for man's good,
    Is since become the hell of flesh and blood.

But grant that there were no eternity;
That life were all, and pleasure life of it:
In sinne's excesse there yet confusions be,
Which spoyle his place, and passionate his wit;
    Making his nature lesse, his reason thrall
    To tyranny of vice vnnaturall.

And as hell-fires, not wanting heat, want light,
So these strange witchcrafts, which like pleasures
    be,
Not wanting faire inticements, want delight,
Inward being nothing but deformity,
    And doe at open doores let fraile powers in
    To that straight bidding Little Ease of sinne.

Is there ought more wonderfull than this—
That man, euen in the state of his perfection,
All things vncurst, nothing yet done amisse,
And so in him no base of his defection,
    Should fall from God, and breake his Maker's
        will,
    Which could haue no end, but to know the ill?

I aske the rather, since in Paradise
Eternity was obiect to his passion,
And hee in goodnesse like his Maker, wise
As from his spirit taking life and fashion;
    What greater power there was to master this,
    Or how a less could worke, my question is?

For who made all, 'tis sure yet could not make
Any aboue himselfe, as princes can,
So as against his will no power could take
A creature from him, nor corrupt a man;
    And yet who thinks he marr'd that made vs good,
    As well may think God lesse than flesh and blood.

Where did our being then seeke out priuation?
Aboue, within, without vs, all was pure;
Onely the angels from their discreation,
By smart declar'd no being was secure,
    But that transcendent goodnesse, which subsists
    By forming and reforming what it lists.

So as within the man there was no more
But possibility to worke upon,
And in these spirits which were faln before
An abstract curst eternity alone;
    Refined by their high places in creation,
    To adde more craft and malice to temptation.

Now with what force upon these middle spheares
Of Probable and Possibility;
Which no one constant demonstration beares,
And so can neither bind, nor bounded be;
    What those could work, that, hauing lost their God,
    Aspire to be our tempters and our rod,

Too well is witness'd by this fall of ours:
For wee, not knowing yet that there was ill,
Gaue easie credit to deceiuing powers,
Who wrought vpon vs onely by our will;
    Perswading, like it, all was to it free,
    Since, where no sinne was, there no law could be.

And as all finite things seeke infinite,
From thence deriuing what beyond them is,
So man was led by charmes of this dark sp'rit,
Which hee could not know till hee did amisse,
    To trust those serpents, who learn'd since they fell,
    Knew more than we did, euen their own made hell:
Which crafty oddes made vs those clouds imbrace,
Where sinne in ambush lay to ouerthrow
Nature, that would presume to fadome grace,
Or could beleeue what God said was not so.
    Sinne, then we knew thee not, and could not hate;
    And now we know thee, now it is too late.

VIII.

O false and treacherous probability,
Enemy of truth, and friend to wickednesse,
With whose bleare eyes opinion learnes to see
Truth's feeble party here, and barrennesse:
    When thou hast thus misled humanity,
    And lost obedience in the pride of wit,
    With reason dar'st thou iudge the Deity,
    And in thy flesh make bold to fashion it?
Vaine thought! the word of power a riddle is,
And till the vayles be rent, the flesh new borne,
Reueales no wonders of that inward blisse,
Which, but where faith is, euery where findes scorne:
    Who therefore censures God with fleshly sp'rit,
    As well in Time may wrap vp Infinite.

IX.

Syon lyes waste, and thy Jerusalem,
O Lord, is falne to vtter desolation:

Against thy prophets and thy holy men
The sinne hath wrought a fatall combination;
    Prophan'd thy name, thy worship ouerthrowne,
    And made thee, liuing Lord, a God vnknowne.

Thy powerfull lawes, thy wonders of creation,
Thy Word incarnate, glorious heauen, darke hell,
Lye shadowed vnder man's degeneration,
Thy Christ still crucifi'd for doing well:
    Impiety, O Lord, sits on thy throne,
    Which makes thee, liuing Light, a God vnknowne.

Man's superstition hath thy truths entomb'd,
His atheisme againe her pomps defaceth;
That sensuall, vnsatiable, vast wombe
Of thy seene Church thy unseene Church disgraceth:
    There liues no truth with them that seem thine owne,
    Which makes thee, liuing Lord, a God vnknowne.

Yet vnto thee, Lord, (mirrour of transgression,)
Wee, who for earthly idols haue forsaken
Thy heauenly Image, (sinlesse pure impression,)
And so in nets of vanity lye taken;
    All desolate, implore that to thine owne,
    Lord, thou no longer liue a God vnknowne.

Yet, Lord, let Israel's plagues be not eternall,
Nor sinne for euer cloud thy sacred mountaines;
Nor with false flames, spirituall but infernall,
Dry vp thy mercies euer-springing fountaines:
    Rather, sweete Jesus, fill vp time, and come,
    To yeeld the sinne her euerlasting doome.

IX.

SIR JOHN HARINGTON.

PSALM CXII.

Who feare the Lord are trewly blest,
    That dewly worke to doe his will:
Great lands are by his seed possesst;
    His howse, his heires, shall prosper still.

With plenty God shall blesse his store,
    And stay his state, that loveth right:
Yf darkenes come, yet evermore
    The Lord shall lend him happy light.

His love, his mercie, hee bestowes
    On him that saves the poore from wrong,
And gives, and lends, and kindnes shewes,
    Yet still discreetly guides his tongue.

His memorie shall ever bide;
    Yea, though in grave his bones be layd,
His foote shall never fayle or slyde;
    No news shall make his hart affrayd.

He putts in God assured trust;
    And trusting so, hee doth suppose
They need not shrink whose cause is just—
    He shall prevayle against his foes.

Hee doth in hast, but not in wast,
    His goods disperse to such as need;
His righteousness shall ever last,
    His praise and honor shall exceed.

The wicked man, when he this seeth,
    That God the good doth love and cherish,
Shall pyne for griefe and gnash his teeth—
    His wicked thoughts with him shall perish.

PSALM CXXXVII.

By Babell's brooks we sitt and weep,
  O Sion, when on thee we think;
Our harps hang'd upp doe sylence keep
  On trees along the river's brink:
Yet they that thralle us thus by wrong,
Amid our sorrowes aske a song.

Come, sing us now a song, say they,
  As once you song at anie hand:
Alasse! how can we sing or play
  Jehovah's songs in strangers' land?
Yet let my hand forgett all playes,
If Salem I forget to praise.

If Salem byde not firm in mynd,
  Let to my roofe my tongue be glew'd,
If other joy then her I finde.
  Lord, think on Edom's race so rude,
That thus that daie did whet this nation,
Root up, root up her strong foundation.

* * * * * * *

X.

MICHAEL DRAYTON.

THE MOST EXCELLENT SONG, WHICH WAS SALOMON'S,

WHEREIN IS DECLARED THE TRUE AND VNFAINED LOUE BETWEENE CHRIST AND HIS CHURCH, CONTAINING VIII. CHAPTERS.

The Fift Chapter.

WITHIN my garden plot,
  Loe, I am present now!
I gathered haue the myrrhe and spice
  That in aboundance growe.

With honey, milke, and wine,
  I haue refresht me here:
Eat, drink, my friends, be mery there,
  With harty friendly cheare.

Although in slumbering sleepe
  It seemes to you I lay,
Yet heare I my beloued knock,
  Methinkes I heare him say:

Open to me the gate,
  My loue, my heart's delight,
For, loe, my locks are all bedewed
  With drizling drops of night.

My garments are put off,
  Then may I not doo so;
Shal I defile my feet I washt
  So white as any snow?

Then fast euen by the dore
  To me he shew'd his hand:
My heart was then enamoured,
  When as I saw him stand.

Then straightwaies vp I rose
  To ope the dore with speed;
My handes and fingers dropped myrrhe
  Vpon the bar indeede.

Then opened I the dore
  Vnto my loue at last;
But all in vain; for why? before
  My loue was gone and past.

There sought I for my loue,
  Then could I crie and call;
But him I could not find, nor he
  Nould answer me at all.

The watchmen found me then,
  As thus I walk'd astray;
They wounded me, and from my head
  My vaile they took away.

Ye daughters of Ierusalem,
  If ye my loue doo see,
Tell him that I am sicke for loue;
  Yea, tel him this from me.

Thou peerelesse gem of price,
  I pray thee to vs tell,
What is thy loue, what may he be,
  That doth so far excell?

In my beloued's face
  The rose and lilly striue;
Among ten thousand men not one
  Is found so faire aliue.

His head like finest gold,
  With secret sweet perfume;

His curled locks hang all as black
  As any rauen's plume.

His eies be like to doues'
  On riuers' banks below,
Ywasht with milk, whose collours are
  Most gallant to the shew.

His cheeks like to a plot
  Where spice and flowers growe;
His lips like to the lilly white,
  From whence pure myrrh doth flow.

His hands like rings of gold
  With costly chrisalet;
His belly like the yuory white,
  With seemly saphyrs set.

His legs like pillers strong
  Of marble set in gold;
His countenance like Libanon,
  Or cedars, to behold.

His mouth it is as sweet,
  Yea, sweet as sweet may be:
This is my loue, ye virgins, loe!
  Euen such a one is he!

Thou fairest of vs all,
  Whether is thy louer gone?
Tell us, and we will goe with thee;
  Thou shalt not goe alone.

THE SONG OF ANNAH

FOR THE BRINGING FOORTH OF SAMUEL HER SONNE.

The Second Chap. of the Firste Booke of Samuel.

My heart doth in the Lord reioice;
  That liuing Lord of might,

Which doth his seruant's horn exalt
  In al his people's sight.

I wil reioice in their despight
  Which erst haue me abhord,
Because that my saluation
  Dependeth on the Lord.

None is so holie as the Lord;
  Besides thee none there are;
With our God there is no God
  That may himselfe compare.

See that no more presumptuously
  Ye neither boast nor vaunt,
Nor yet vnseemly speak such things
  So proud and arrogant.

For why? the counsell of the Lord
  In depth cannot be sought:
Our enterprises and our actes
  By him to passe are brought.

The bowe is broke, the mightie ones
  Subuerted are at length,
And they which weak and feeble were
  Increased are in strength.

They that were ful and had great store,
  With labor buy their bread;
And they which hungrie were and poore,
  With plentie now are fed:

So that the wombe which barren was
  Hath many children born,
And she which store of children had
  Is left now all forlorne.

The Lord doth kill and make aliue,
  His iudgments all are iust;
He throweth downe into the graue,
  And raiseth from the dust.

The Lord doth make both rich and poore;
  He al our thoughts doth trie;
He bringeth low, and eke again e
  Exalteth vp on hie.

He raiseth vp the simple soule
  Whom men pursude with hate,
To sit amongst the mightie ones
  In chaire of princely state.

For why? the pillers of the earth
  He placed with his hand,
Whose mighty strength doth stil support
  The waight of al the land.

He wil preserue his saints; likewise
  The wicked men at length
He wil confound: let no man seem
  To glory in his strength.

The enemies of God the Lord
  Shall be destroied al;
From heauen he shal thunder send,
  That on their heads shal fall.

The mightie Lord shall iudge the world,
  And giue his power alone
Vnto the king; and shal exalt
  His owne annointed one.

THE PRAIER OF IEREMIAH,

BEWAILING THE CAPTIUITIE OF THE PEOPLE.

In the fift Chap. of his Lamentations.

CAL vnto mind, Oh mightie Lord,
  The wrongs we daily take;
Consider and behold the same
  For thy great mercies' sake.

Our lands and our inheritance
  Meere strangers do possesse;
The alients in our houses dwel,
  And we without redresse.

We now, alas! are fatherlesse,
  And stil pursude with hate;
Our mourning mothers now remaine
  In wofull widdowes' state.

We buy the water which we drink,
  Such is our grievous want:
Likewise the wood euen for our vse
  That we ourselues did plant.

Our neckes are subiect to the yoke
  Of persecution's thrall;
We, wearied out with cruell toile,
  Can find no rest at all.

Afore time we in Egypt land
  And in Assyria serued,
For food our hunger to sustaine,
  Least that we should haue sterued.

Our fathers which are dead and gone
  Haue sinned wondrous sore;
And we now scourg'd for their offence—
  Ah! woe are we therefore.

Those seruile slaues which bondmen be,
  Of them in fear we stand:
Yet no man doth deliuer vs
  From cruel caitiues' hand.

Our liuings we are forced to get
  In perils of our liues;
The drie and barren wildernesse
  Therto by danger driues.

Our skins be scorcht, as though they had
  Bin in an ouen dride,

With famine and the penury
  Which here we doo abide.
Our wiues and maides defloured are
  By violence and force,
On Sion and in Iuda land,
  Sans pity or remorce.

Our kings by cruel enimies
  With cordes are hanged vp;
Our grauest, sage, and ancient men,
  Haue tasted of that cup.

Our yoong men they haue put to sword,
  Not one at al they spare:
Our litle boyes vpon the tree
  Sans pitie hanged are.

Our elders sitting in the gates
  Can now no more be found;
Our youth leaue off to take delight
  In musick's sacred sound.

The ioy and comfort of our heart
  Away is fled and gone;
Our solace is with sorrow mixt,
  Our mirth is turn'd to mone.

Our glory now is laid full low,
  And buried in the ground;
Our sins full sore do burthen vs,
  Whose greatnes doth abound.

Oh, holy blessed Sion hill,
  My heart is woe for thee:
Mine eies poure foorth a flood of teares
  This dismal day to see:

Which art destroied, and now lieth wast
  From sacred vse and trade;
Thy holie place is now a den
  Of filthy foxes made.

But thou, the euerliuing Lord,
   Which doost remaine for aye,
Whose seat aboue the firmament
   Full sure and still doth stay,—

Wherefore dost thou forsake thine own?
   Shall we forgotten be?
Turn vs, good Lord, and so we shall
   Be turned vnto thee.

Lord, call vs home from our exile
   To place of our abode;
Thou long inough hast punisht vs—
   Oh Lord, now spare thy rod.

A SONG OF MOSES AND THE ISRAELITES,

FOR THEIR DELIUERANCE OUT OF EGYPT.

The XV. Chap. of Exodus.

I WILL sing praise vnto the Lord for aie,
Who hath triumphed gloriously alone;
The horse and rider he hath ouerthrowen
And swallowed vp, euen in the raging sea.

He is my strength; he is my song of praise;
He is the God of my saluation:
A temple will I build to him alone—
I will exalt my fathers' God alwaies.

The Lord Iehouah is a man of warre:
Pharoe, his chariots, and his mightie hoste
Were by his hand in the wilde waters lost,
His captaines drowned in Red Sea so farre.

Into the bottom there they sanke like stones,
The mightie depthes our enemies deuour:
Thy owne right hand is gloorious in thy power,
Thy owne right hand hath bruised all their bones.

And in thy glorie thou subuerted hast
The rebels rising to resist thy power;
Thou sentst thy wrath, which shall them all deuour,
Euen as the fire doth the stubble wast.

And with a blast out of thy nostrilles
The flowing flood stood still as any stone;
The waters were congealed all in one,
And firme and sure as any rockes or hilles.

The furious foe so vainly vaunteth stil,
And voweth to pursue with endlesse toile,
And not return till he haue got the spoile;
With fire and sword they wil destroy and kill.

Thou sentst the wind which ouerwhelm'd them all,
The surging seas came sousing in againe:
As in the water, so with might and maine,
Like lead, vnto the bottome downe they fall.

Oh, mightie Lord, who may with thee compare?
Amongst the gods I find none like to thee,
Whose glorie's in holines, whose feares in praises
    be,
Whose chiefe delights in working woonders are.

Thou stretchest out thy right and holy arme,
And presently the earth did them deuour;
And thou wilt bring vs by thy mightie power,
As thou hast promist, without further harme.

And for thy people, Lord, thou shalt prouide
A place and seat of quietnesse and rest:
The nations all with feare shall be opprest,
And Palestina quake for all her pride.

The dukes of Edom shal hang downe the head;
The Moabites shall tremble then for feare;
The Cananites in presence shall appeare
Like vnto men whose fainting heartes were dead.

And feare and dread shall fall on them, alas!
Because thou helpest with thy mightie hand;
So stil as stones amazed they shal stand,
Oh mightie Lord, while thine elect doo passe.

And thou shalt bring thy chosen and elect
Unto the mount of thine inheritance,
A place prepared thy people to aduance:
A sanctuary there thou shalt erect;
Which thou, O Lord, establish'd hast therefore,
And there thy name shal raigne for euermore.

A SONG OF THE FAITHFULL FOR THE MERCIES OF GOD.

In the XII. Chap. of the prophesie of Isaiah.

OH liuing Lord, I still will laude thy name!
  For though thou wert offended once with mee,
Thy heauy wrath is turn'd from me againe,
  And graciously thou now doost comfort mee.

Behold, the Lord is my saluation,
  I trust in him, and feare not any power:
He is my song, the strength I lean vpon;
  The Lord God is my louing Sauiour.

Wherefore with ioy out of the well of life
  Draw foorth sweet water which it dooth affoord:
And in the day of trouble and of strife
  Cal on the name of God the liuing Lord.

Extol his works and woonders to the sunne,
  Unto al people let his praise be showne;
Record in song the meruails he hath done,
  And let his glorie through the world be blowne.

Crie out aloud and shout on Sion hill;
  I giue thee charge that this proclaimed be,—
The great and mightie King of Israëll
  Now only dwelleth in the midst of thee.

A SONG OF THE FAITHFULL.

In the third Chap. of the prophesie of Habacucke.

Lord, at thy voice my heart for feare hath trembled;
Vnto the world, Lord, let thy workes be showen:
In these our daies now let thy power be knowen,
And yet in wrath let mercie be remembred.

From Teman, loe, our God you may behold,
The Holie One from Paran mount so hie;
His glorie hath cleane couered the skie,
And in the earth his praises be inrolde.

His shining was more clearer than the light,
And from his hands a fulnesse did proceed,
Which did contain his wrath and power indeed:
Consuming plagues and fire were in his sight.

He stood aloft and compassed the land,
And of the nations doth defusion make;
The mountaines rent, the hilles for feare did quake,—
His vnknown pathes no man may vnderstand.

The Morians' tentes euen for their wickednes
I might behold, the land of Midian
Amaz'd and trembling, like vnto a man
Forsaken quite, and left in great distresse.

What, did the riuers moue the Lord to ire?
Or did the floods his Maiesty displease?
Or was the Lord offended with the seas,
That thou camest forth in chariot hot as fire?

Thy force and power thou freely didst relate;
Vnto the tribes thy oath doth surely stand;
And by thy strength thou didst diuide the land,
And from the earth the riuers separate.

The mountaines saw and trembled for feare,
The sturdy streame with speed foorth passed by;
The mighty depthes shout out a hideous crie,
And then aloft their waues they did vpreare.

The sun and moon amid their course stood still,
The speares and arrowes forth with shining went;
Thou spoilest the land, being to anger bent,
And in displeasure thou didst slay and kill.

Thou wentest foorth for thine owne chosen's
  sake,
For the sauegard of thine annointed one;
The house of wicked men is ouerthrowne,
And their foundations now goe all to wracke.

Their townes thou strikest by thy mightie power
With their own weapons, made for their defence,
Who like a whyrlwind came with the pretence
The poore and simple man quite to deuoure.

Thou madest thy horse on seas to gallop fast;
Vpon the waues thou ridest here and there:
My intrals trembled then for verie feare,
And at thy voice my lips shooke at the last.

Griefe pierc'd my bones, and feare did me annoy,
In time of trouble where I might find rest:
For to reuenge when once the Lord is prest,
With plagues he wil the people quite destroy.

The fig-tree now no more shall sprout nor flou-
  rish;
The pleasant vine no more with grapes abound;
No pleasure in the citie shall be found,
The field no more her fruit shal feed nor nourish.

The sheep shall now be taken from the fold;
In stall of bullocks there shall be no choice:
Yet in the Lord my Sauiour I reioice;
My hope in God yet wil I surely hold.

God is my strength, the Lord my only stay;
My feet for swiftnesse it is he will make
Like to the hind's, who none in course can take:
Vpon high places he will make me way.

THE SONG OF IONAH IN THE WHALE'S BELLIE.

In the Second Chap. of Ionah.

In griefe and anguish of my heart
  My voice I did extend
Unto the Lord, and he thereto
  A willing eare did lend.

Euen from the deep and darkest pit,
  And the infernall lake,
To me he hath bow'd down his eare,
  For his great mercies' sake.

For thou into the middest
  Of surging seas so deepe
Hast cast me foorth, whose bottom is
  So low and woondrous steep:

Whose mighty wallowing waues,
  Which from the floods do flow,
Haue with their power vp swallowed me,
  And ouerwhelm'd me tho.

Then said I,—Loe I am exilde
  From presence of thy face!
Yet wil I once againe behold
  Thy house and dwelling-place.

The waters haue encompast me,
  The floods inclosde me round,
The weeds haue sore encombred me,
  Which in the seas abound.

Vnto the valeyes down I went,
  Beneath the hils which stand;
The earth hath there enuiron'd me
  With force of al the land.

Yet hast thou stil preserued me
  From all these dangers here,
And brought my life out of the pit,
  Oh Lord, my God so deare.

My soule consuming thus with care,
  I praied vnto the Lord;
And he from out his holie place
  Heard me with one accord.

Who to vain lieng vanities
  Doth whollie him betake
Doth erre; also God's mercie he
  Doth vtterly forsake.

But I wil offer vnto him
  The sacrifice of praise;
And pay my vowes, ascribing thanks
  Vnto the Lord alwaies.

THE FINDING OF MOSES.

Now Pharaoh's daughter Termuth young and faire,
With such choyce maydens as she fauor'd most,
Needes would abroad to take the gentle ayre,
Whilst the rich yeere his braueries seem'd to boast.
Softly she walkes downe to the sacred flood,
Through the calme shades most peaceable and quiet,
In the cool streames to check the pampred blood,
Stird with strong youth and their delicious diet.
Such as the princesse, such the day addressed,
As though prouided equally to paire her,
Either in other fortunately blessed,
She by the day, the day by her made fairer;

THE FINDING OF MOSES.

Both in the height and fulnesse of their pleasure,
As to them both some future good diuining,
Holding a steadie and accomplish'd measure;
This in her perfect clearnesse, that in shining.
The very ayre, to emulate her meekenesse,
Stroue to be bright and peaceable as she,
That it grew iealous of that sodaine sleekenesse,
Fearing it ofter otherwise might be.
And if the fleet winde by some rigorous gale
Seem'd to be mou'd, and patiently to chide her,
It was as angry with her lawnie vaile,
That from his sight it enuiously should hide her.
And now approching to the flowrie meade,
Where the rich summer curiously had dight her,
(See this most blessed, this vnusual hap,)
Which seem'd in all her iollitie arayde,
With nature's cost and pleasures to delight her,
She the small basket sooner should espie,
That the child wak'd, and missing of his pap,
As for her succour, instantly did cry.
Forth of the flagges she caus'd it to be taken,
Calling her maids this orphanet to see:
Much did she ioy an innocent forsaken
By her from peril priuiledgd might be.
This sweet princesse, most pittifull and milde,
Soone on her knee vnswathes it as her owne,
Found for a man so beautifull a childe,
Might for an Hebrew easily be knowne:
Noting the care in dressing it bestow'd,
Each thing that fitted gentlenesse to weare,
Iudg'd the sad parents this lost infant ow'd
Were as invulgar as their fruit was faire.
Saith she, "My minde not any way suggests
An vnchaste wombe these lineaments hath bred;
For thy faire brow apparently contests
The currant stamp of a cleane nuptial bed."

She named it Moyses, which in time might tell
(For names doe many mysteries expound)
When it was young the chance that it befell,
How by the water strangely it was found.

THE PASSAGE OF THE RED SEA.

Those which at home scorn'd Pharaoh and his
 force,
And whose departure he did humbly pray,
He now pursues with his Egyptian horse
And warlike foote, to spoile them on the way.
Where his choice people strongly to protect,
The only God of emperie and of might,
Before his host his standard doth erect,
A glorious pillar in a field of light;
Which he by day in sable doth vnfolde,
To dare the sunne his ardour to forbeare,
By night conuerts it into flaming golde,
Away the coldnesse of the same to feare.
Not by Philistia he his force will leade,
Though the farre nearer and the happier way:
His men of warre a glorious march shall tread
On the vast bowels of the bloudie sea;
And sends the windes as currers forth before
To make them way from Pharaoh's power to flie,
And to conuey them to a safer shore.
Such is his might that can make oceans drie,
Which by the stroke of that commanding wand
Shouldred the rough seas forcibly together,
Raised as rampiers by that glorious hand,
(Twixt which they march,) that did conduct them
 thither.
The surly waues their Ruler's will obay'd,
By him made vp in this confused masse,
Like as an ambush secretly were laid,

PASSAGE OF THE RED SEA.

To set on Pharaoh as his power should passe,
Which soone with wombes insatiably wide,
Loos'd from their late bounds by the Almightie's
    power,
Come raging in, enclosing euery side,
And the Egyptians instantly deuour.
The sling, the stiffe bowe, and the sharpned launce,
Floating confusdly on the waters rude,
They which these weapons lately did aduance,
Perish in sight of them that they pursude:
Clashing of armours and the rumorous sound
Of the sterne billowes in contention stood,
Which to the shores doe euery way rebound,
As doth affright the monsters of the flood.
Death is discern'd triumphantly in armes,
On the rough seas his slaughterie to keepe,
And his colde selfe in breath of mortals warmes
Vpon the dimpled bosome of the deepe.
There might you see a checkquer'd ensigne swim
About the bodie of the enui'd dead,
Serue for a hearse or couerture to him
Ere while did waft it proudly 'bout his head:
The warlike chariot turn'd vpon the backe,
With the dead horses in their traces tide,
Drags their fat carkasse through the foamie
    bracke,
That drew it late vndauntedly in pride.
There floats the bar'd steed with his rider drown'd,
Whose foot in his caparison is cast,
Who late with sharpe spurs did his courser
    wound,
Himselfe now ridden with his strangled beast.
The waters conquer (without helpe of hand)
For them to take, for which they neuer toile,
And like a quarrie cast them on the land,
As those they slew they left to them to spoile.

In eightie-eight[1] at Douer that had beene
To view that nauie (like a mighty wood)
Whose sailes swept heauen, might eas'lie there
    haue seene
How puissant Pharaoh perish'd in the floud.
What for a conquest strictly they did keepe,
Into the channel presently was pour'd;
Castilian riches scatter'd on the deepe,
That Spaine's long hopes had sodainly deuour'd.
Th' afflicted English rang'd along the strand,
To waite what would this threatening power betide,
Now when the Lord with a victorious hand
In his high iustice scourg'd the Iberian pride.

THE LAW GIVEN ON SINAI.

Now when to Sina they approched neare,
God calls vp Moyses to the mount aboue,
And all the rest commaundeth to forbeare,
Nor from the bounds assign'd them to remoue.
For who those limits loosely did exceede,
Which were by Moyses mark'd them out beneath,
The Lord had irreuocably decreed
With darts or stones should surely die the death:
Where as the people in a wondrous fright,
(With hearts transfixed euen with frosen blood)
Beheld their leader openly in sight
Passe to the Lord, where he in glory stood.
Thunder and lightning led him down the ayre,
Trumpets celestial sounding as he came,
Which struck the people with astounding feare,
Himselfe inuested in a splendorous flame.
Sina before him fearfully did shake,

---

[1] 1598.

Couer'd all ouer in a smouldering smoake,
As ready the foundation to forsake,
On the dread presence of the Lord to looke.
Erect your spirits, and lend attentiue ear,
To marke at Sina what to you is said.
Weake Moyses now you shall not simply heare,
The son of Amram and of Iacobed;
But He that Adam did imparadise,
And lent him comfort in his proper blood,
And saued Noah, that did the arke deuise,
When the old world else perish'd in the flood;
To righteous Abraham Canaan franckly lent,
And brought forth Isaac so extreamly late,
Jacob so faire and many children sent,
And rais'd chast Joseph to so high estate;
He whose iust hand plagu'd Egypt for your sake,
That Pharaoh's power so scornefully did mock,
Way for his people through the sea did make,
Gaue food from Heauen and water from the rock.
Whilst Moyses now in this cloud-couered hill
Full forty dayes his pure aboade did make,
Whilst that great God, in his almighty will,
With him of all his ordinances spake:
The decalogue from which religion tooke
The being; sinne and righteousnesse began
The different knowledge, and the certaine booke
Of testimony betwixt God and man:
The ceremoniall as judicious lawes,
From his high wisdome that receiu'd their ground,
Not to be altred in the smallest clause,
But, as their Maker, wondrously profound.
The composition of that sacred phane,
Which as a symbol curiously did shew,
What all his six daye's workmanship containe,
Whose perfect modell his owne finger drew.

XI.

HENRY LOK.

PSALME XXVII.

The Lord! he is my saving light,
  Whom should I therefore feare?
He makes my foes to fall, whose teeth
  Would me in sunder teare.

Though hostes of men besiege my soule,
  My heart shall neuer dread;
So that within his court and sight,
  My life may still be led.

For in his Church from trouble free
  He shall me keepe in holde;
In spight of foes, his wrondrous prayse
  My song shall still unfold.

Have mercie, Lord, therefore, on me,
  And heare me when I cry;
Thou bidst me looke with hope on thee;
  For help to thee I fly.

In wrath therefore hide not thy face,
  But be thou still my aide;
Though parents fayle thou wilt assist—
  Thy promise so hath said.

Teach me thy truth, and thy right path,
  Least that the enemy
Prevaile against my life; whose tongues
  Entrap me treacherously.

My heart would fainte for feare, unless
  My faith did build on thee;
My hope's my God, and comfort's strength,
  Who will deliver me.

PSALME CXXI.

Vnto the hils I lift my eyes,
  From whence my helpe shall grow;
Euen to the Lord which fram'd the heauens,
  And made the deeps below.

He will not let my feete to slip;
  My watchman neither sleepes:
Behold the Lord of Israell still
  His flocke in safety keepes.

The Lord is my defence; he doth
  About me shadow cast;
By day nor night the sunne nor moone
  My limbs shall burne or blast.

He shall preserue me from all ill,
  And me from sinne protect;
My going-in, and comming forth,
  He euer shall direct.

A VERSION OF THE LORD'S PRAYER.

Our Father which in heauen art,
  Lorde! hallowed be thy name:
Thy kingdome come, thy will be done,
  In heauen and earth the same.

Giue us this day our daily bread;
  Our trespasses forgiue,
As we for other men's offence
  Doe freely pardon giue.

Into temptation leade us not,
  But 'liuer us from ill;
For thine all kingdome, glory, powre,
  Is now, and euer will.

AVARICE.

> Who loueth gold shall lacke, and he
>   Who couets much want store:
> With wealth charge growes; the owner but
>   Increaseth paine the more.

WHAT though the world, through baleful lust of
    gold,
Be thus transported with a greedy mind,
To purchase wealth, which makes the coward bold
To search land, sea, and hell, the same to find?
    Yet as it doth increase, so doth desire,
    And soone consume as oyle amidst the fire.

A iust reward of so vnworthy trade
As doth debase nobilitie of soule,
Which, made immortal, scornes those things that
    vade,
And in the wise should earthly effects controule.
    But mould-warp like, these blindfold grope in
        vaine:
    Vaine their desires; more vaine the fruit they
        gaine.

If honor, wealth, and calling do excell
The common sort, so charge doth grow with all:
Few with a little sure may liue as well,
As many may, though greater wealth befall:
    It is not wealth to haue of goods great store,
    But wealth to be suffised, and need no more.

Who hath aboundance and it vseth well,
Is but a steward to his family;
A purse-bearer for such as neare him dwell;
An amner to the poore that helpless cry:
    He but his share doth spend, though somewhat
        better,
    And what he leaues he is to world a detter.

THE MISERABLE STATE OF THE WICKED.

> Who feares not God shall not escape,
> His daies as shadows pas;
> Though wicked men triumph sometimes,
> And iust men waile, alas!

WHEN as contrariwise the wicked one
Shall be dismounted from his seat of trust,
Dismayd and desolate, forlorne, alone,
Pursued by heauen and earth, by iudgment iust,
   Of God and man forsaken and contemnd,
   As be the innocent before condemnd:

The pompe and glory of his passed pride
Like to a flower shall vanish and decay;
His life like ruines downe shall headlong slide,
His fame like to a shadow vade away.
   Because he feared not the God of might,
   In iustice shall these woes vpon him light.

And yet in truth it is a wondrous case
To see the iust so many woes sustaine:
Not that I thinke that pitie can haue place
With wicked ones to make them wrong refraine;
   But that the God of iustice doth permit
   His seruants to be subiect vnto it.

For you shall lightly see the better man
The more afflicted in his worldly state;
The vilest person, worst, that find you can,
Most wealthy and loued most, though worthy hate:
   But it is vaine to search God's mind herein—
   Thereof to descant I will not begin.

SONNETS FROM THE "FIRST CENTURIE OF SONETS."

SONET XLIIIII.

My wicked flesh, O Lord, with sin full fraight,
  Whose eye doth lust for euerie earthly thing,
  By couetise allurde, hath bit the baight
  That me to Satan's seruitude will bring.
By violence I vertue's right would wring
  Out of possession of the soule so weake,
  Like vineyard which the wicked Achab king
  Possest by tirant's power, which lawes do breake.
Let prophets thine, Lord, to my soule so speake,
  That in repentant sackcloth I may mone
  The murther of thy grace which I did wreake,
  Whilst to my natiue strength I trust alone:
    And let my Sauiour so prolong my daies,
    That henceforth I may turne from sinfull waies.

SONET LI.

Whilst in the garden of this earthly soile
  Myself to solace and to bath I bend,
  And fain would quench sin's heat, which seems to boile
  Amidst my secret thoughts, which shadow lend:
My sence and reasons which should me defend,
  As iudges chosen to the common weale,
  Allur'd by lust, my ruine do pretend
  By force of sin, which shamelesse they reueale:
They secretly on my affections steale,
  When modestie my maides I sent away,
  To whom for helpe I thought I might appeale,
  But grace yet strengthens me to say them nay:
    Yet they accuse me, Lord, and die I shall,
    If Christ my Daniell be not iudge of all.

SONET LIII.

A HUSBANDMAN within thy Church by grace
I am, O Lord, and labour at the plough;
My hand holds fast, ne will I turne my face
From following thee, although the soile be
  rough.
The loue of world doth make it seeme more tough,
  And burning lust doth scorch in heat of day,
  Till fainting, faith would seeke delightfull bough
  To shade my soule from danger of decay.
But yet in hope of grace from thee I stay,
  And do not yeeld, although my courage quaile:
  To rescue me beprest I do thee pray,
  If sinfull death do seeke me to assaile.
    Let me runne forth my race vnto the end,
    Which by thy helpe, O Lord, I do intend.

SONNETS FROM THE "SECOND CENTURIE."

SONET XXVII.

So blinde, O Lord, haue my affections bin,
  And so deceitfull hath bin Satan's slight,
  That to giue credit I did first begin
  To pride and lust, as heauenly powers of might:
I offred all my sences with delight,
  A sacrifice to feede those idols vaine:
  Of all the presents proffred day and night,
  Nought vnconsumde I saw there did remaine,
Till that thy prophets by thy word made plaine
  The falshood by the which I was deceiued;
  How Satan's kingdome made hereof a gaine,
  And wickednesse my hope and faith bereaued.
    But now the sifted ashes of thy word
    Bewraies Bel's prists, slaies dragon without
      sword.

SONET LXXXI.

Lo, how I groueling vnder burden lie
Of sin, of shame, of feare, Lord, of thy sight;
My guilt so manifold dare not come nie
Thy throne of mercy, mirror of thy might.
With hidden and with ignorant sinnes I fight,
  Dispairing and presumptuous faults also:
  All fleshly frailtie on my backe doth light,
  Originall and actuall with me go.
Against a streame of lusts my will would roe
  To gaine the shoare of grace, the port of peace:
But flouds of foule affections ouerfloe,
And sinke I must; I see now no release,
    Vnlesse my Sauiour deare this burden take,
    And faith a ship of safetie for me make.

SONET XC.

On sweete and sauorie bread of wholesome kinde,
Which in thy word thou offrest store to me,
To feed vpon the flesh doth lothing finde,
And leaues to leane, O Lord, alone on thee:
The leauen of the Pharisees will bee
  The surfet of my soule, and death in fine,
  Which, coueting to tast forbidden tree,
  To carnall rules and reasons doth incline.
So lauishly my lusts do tast the wine
  Which sowrest grapes of sin filles in my cup,
That, lo, my teeth now set on edge I pine,
Not able wholesome food to swallow vp,
    Vnlesse thou mend my tast, and hart doest frame
    To loue thy lawes, and praise thy holy name.

XII.

WILLIAM HUNNIS.

PSALME VI.

Domine, ne in furore. The first Part.

O Lord, when I myself behold,
  How wicked I haue bin,
And view the paths and waies I went,
  Wandring from sin to sin;

Againe to thinke vpon thy power,
  Thy iudgement and thy might;
And how that nothing can be hid,
  Or close kept from thy sight;.

Euen then, alas! I shake and quake,
  And tremble where I stand,
For feare thou shouldst reuenged be
  By power of wrathful hand.

The weight of sinne is verie great;
  For this to mind I call,
That one proud thought made angels once
  From heauen to slide and fall.

Adam likewise, and Eve his wife,
  For breaking thy precept,
From Paradise expelled were,
  And death thereby hath crept

Vpon them both, and on their seede,
  For euer to remaine,
But that by faith in Christ thy Sonne
  We hope to liue againe.

The earth not able was to beare,
  But quicke did swallow in,
Corah, Dathan, and Abiron,
  By reason of their sin.

Also because king David did
  His people number all,
Thou, Lord, therefore, in three daies' space,
  Such grieuous plague letst fall,

That seuentie thousand men forthwith
  Thereof dyde presentlie;
Such was thy worke, such was thy wrath,
  Thy mightie power to trie.

Alas! my sins surmounteth theirs,
  Mine cannot numbred bee;
And from thy wrath, most mightie God,
  I knowe not where to flee.

If into heauen I might ascend,
  Where angels thine remaine,
O Lord, thy wrath would thrust me forth
  Downe to the earth againe.

And in the earth here is no place
  Of refuge to be found,
Nor in the deepe, and water-course
  That passeth vnder ground.

Vouchsafe therefore, I thee beseech,
  On me some mercie take,
And turne thy wrath from me awaie,
  For Jesus Christe's sake.

[1]*Lord, in thy wrath reprove me not,*
  Ne chast me in thine ire;
But with thy mercie shadowe me,
  I humblie thee desire.

---

[1] Verse 1. *Domine, ne in furore tuo arguas me: neq' in ira tua corripias me.*

PSALM VI.

I know it is my grieuous sinnes
  That doo thy wrath prouoke:
But yet, O Lord, in rigour thine
  Forbeare thy heauie stroke;

And rather with thy mercie sweete
  Behold my heauie plight;
How weake and feeble I appeare
  Before thy blessed sight.

For nature mine corrupted is,
  And wounded with the dart
Of lust and foule concupiscence,
  Throughout in eu'rie part.

I am in sinne conceiu'd and borne,
  The child of wrath and death,
Hauing but here a little time
  To liue and drawe my breath.

I feele myselfe still apt and prone
  To wickednesse and vice,
And drowned thus in sinne I lie,
  And haue no power to rise.

[2] *It is thy mercie, O sweet Christ,*
  That must my health restore;
For all my bones are troubled much,
  And vexed verie sore.

I am not able to withstand
  Temptations such as bee:
Wherefore, good Lord, vouchsafe to heale
  My great infirmitie.

Good Christ, as thou to Peter didst,
  Reach forth thy hand to me,

---

[2] Verse 2. *Miserere mei, Domine, quoniam infirmus sum: sana me, Domine, quoniam conturbata sunt omnia ossa mea.*

When he upon the water went,
  There drowned like to be.

And as the leaper clensed was.
  By touching with thy hand;
And Peter's mother raised up
  From feuer whole to stand:

So let that hand of mercie thine
  Make cleane the leprosie
Of lothsome lust vpon me growne
  Through mine iniquitie.

Then shal there strength in me appere,
  Through grace, my chiefe reliefe;
Thy death, O Christ, the medicine is
  That helpeth all my griefe.

[1] *My soule is troubled verie sore*
  By reason of my sin:
But, Lord, how long shall I abide
  Thus sorrowfull therein?

I doubt not, Lord, but thou, which hast
  My stonie hart made soft,
With willing mind thy grace to craue
  From time to time so oft,

Wilt not now stay, but forth proceed
  My perfect health to make:
Although awhile thou doost deferre,
  Yet is it for my sake.

For, Lord, thou knowst our nature such,
  If we great things obtaine,
And in the getting of the same
  Do feel no griefe or paine;

---

[1] Verse 3. *Et anima mea conturbata est valde: sed tu Domine vsquequo?*

We little doo esteeme thereof:
  But, hardly brought to passe,
A thousand times we doe esteeme
  Much more then th' other was.

So, Lord, if thou shouldst at the first
  Grant my petition,
The greatnes of offenses mine
  I should not thinke vpon.

Wherefore my hope still bids me cry
  With faithfull hart in brest;
As did the faithful Cananite,
  Whose daughter was possest.

At least, if I still knock and call
  Vpon thy holie name,
At length thou wilt heare my request,
  And grant to me the same:

As did the man three loaues of bread
  Vnto his neighbour lend,
Whose knocking long forst him to rise,
  And shew himselfe a frend.

Lord, by the mouth of thy deare Son
  This promise didst thou make,
That if we knocke, thou open wilt
  The doore euen for his sake.

Wherefore we crie, we knock, we call,
  And neuer cease will wee,
Till thou doo turne to vs, O Lord,
  That we may turne to thee.

PSALME LI.

Miserere mei. The first Part.

1 O THOU, that madst the world of nought,
     Whom God thy creatures call;
   Which formedst man like to thyself,
     Yet suffredst him to fall:

2 Thou God, which by thy heauenlie word
    Didst fleshe of virgin take,
  And so becamst both God and man,
    For sinful fleshe's sake:

3 O thou, that sawest when man by sinne
    To hell was ouerthrowne,
  Didst meeklie suffer death on crosse,
    To haue thy mercies knowne:

4 Thou God, which didst the patriarks
    And fathers old diuine
  From time to time preserue and keepe
    By mercies great of thine:

5 O thou, that Noah kepts from floud,
    And Abram daie by daie,
  As he along through Ægypt past,
    Didst guide him in the waie:

6 Thou God, that Lot from Sodom's plague
    Didst safelie keepe also,
  And Daniel from the lions' iawes,
    Thy mercie great to shew:

7 O thou good God, that didst diuide
    The sea like hils to stand,
  That children thine might thorough pas
    From cruell Pharoe's hand;

8 So that when Pharoe and his host
    Thy children did pursue,
  Thou ouerthrewst them in the sea,
    To prooue thy saiengs true:

9 O thou, that Ionas in the fish
    Three daies didst keepe from paine,
  Which was a figure of thy death
    And rising vp againe:

PSALM LI.

10 I say, thou God, which didst preserue
    Amidst the fierie flame
  The three young men which sang therein
    The glories of thy name :—

11 [1]*Thou, God, haue mercie on my soule,*
    Thy goodnesse me restore,
  And for thy mercies infinite
    Thinke on my sinne no more.

12 O Lord, the number of my sinnes
    Is more than can be told;
  Wherefore I humblie doo desire
    Thy mercies manifold.

13 For small offense thy mercie small
    May soone small faultes suffice;
  But I, alas! for manie faults
    For greater mercie cries.

14 And though the number of my sins
    Surpasseth salt sea land,
  And that the filth of them deserue
    The wrath of thy iust hand;

15 Yet doo thy mercies farre surmount
    The sinnes of all in all;
  Thou wilt with mercie vs relieue,
    For mercie when we call.

16 Right well I knowe man hath not power
    So much for to transgresse,
  As thou with mercie maist forgiue
    Through thine almightinesse.

17 I doo confesse my faultes be more
    Than thousands else beside,

---

[1] Verse 1. *Miserere mei, Deus, secundum magnam misericordiam tuam; et secundum multitudinem miserationum tuarum dele iniquitatem meam.*

More noisome, and more odious,
   More fowler to be tride,
18 Than euer was the lothsome swine—

*   *   *   *   *   *   *

19 Wherefore, good Lord, doo not behold
   How wicked I haue bin;
 [1]*But wash me from my wickednesse,*
   And clense me from my sin.

20 The Israelites, being defil'd,
   Durst not approach thee nie,
Till they their garments and themselues
   Had washed decentlie.

21 The priests also eke clensed were
   Ere they thy face would see;
Else had they perisht in their sinne—
   Such Lord was thy decree.

22 Alas! how much more need I then
   To craue while I am heere,
To wash my foule and spotted soule,
   That it may cleane appeare!

23 Polluted cloths with filth distaind
   Doe manie washings craue,
Ere that the launder can obteine
   The thing that he would haue.

24 My soule likewise, alas! dooth need
   The manie dewes of grace,
Ere it be cleane; for cankred sinne
   So deepe hath taken place.

25 The leprosie that Naaman had
   Could not be done away,
Till he seuen times in Iordan floud
   Had washt him day by day.

---

[1] Verse 2. *Amplius lava mea ab iniquitate mea, et a peccato meo munda me.*

26 How manie waters need I then
   For to be washed in,
Ere I be purged faire and cleane,
   And clensed from my sin!

27 But, Lord, thy mercie is the sope,
   And washing lee also,
That shall both scowre and clense the filth
   Which in my soule doe grow.

28 Why should I then, alas! despaire
   Of goodness thine to mee,
When that thy iustice willeth me
   To put my trust in thee?

29 Thy promise, Lord, thy mouth hath past,
   Which cannot be but true,
That thou wilt mercie haue on them
   That turne to thee anew.

30 I know, when heauen and earth shall passe,
   This promise shall stand fast:
Wherefore vnto thy Maiestie
   I offer now at last

31 An hart contrite and sorrowfull
   With all humilitie,
For heinous sinnes by it conceiu'd
   Through mine iniquitie.

32 [2]*I doo acknowledge all my faultes;*
   My sinnes stand me before;
I haue them in remembrance, Lord,
   And will for euermore.

33 Because thou shouldst the same forget,
   I still doo thinke thereon,
And set it vp before my face,
   Alwaies to look vpon.

---

[2] Verse 3. *Quoniam iniquitatem meam ego cognosco, et peccatum meum contra me est semper.*

CERTAINE SHORT AND PITHY PRAIERS VNTO IESU CHRIST OUR SAUIOUR.

I.

O IESU sweet, grant that thy grace
　Alwaies so worke in mee,
I may desire the thing to doo
　Most pleasing vnto thee.

O Iesu meeke, thy will be mine,
　My will be thine also;
And that my will may follow thine
　In pleasure, paine, and wo;

O Iesu, what is good for mee,
　I say best known to thee:
Therefore according to thy will
　Haue mercie now on mee.

II.

O IESU, if thou do withdrawe
　Thy comfort for a time,
Let not despaire take hold on mee
　For anie sinnfull crime.

But giue me patience to abide
　Thy pleasure and thy will:
For sure thy iudgments all are right,
　Though I be wicked still.

But yet a promise hast thou made
　To all that trust in thee:
According to which promise, Lord,
　Haue mercie now on me.

III.

O IESU, oft it greeueth me,
　And troubleth sore my mind,

That I so weake and fraile am found,
  To wander with the blind.
O Iesu deare, thou lasting light,
  Whose brightnesse doth excell,
The clearnes of thy beames send downe,
  Within my heart to dwell.
O Iesu, quicken thou my soule,
  That it may cleaue to thee,
And for thy painefull passion sake
  Haue mercie now on me.

A LAMENTATION TOUCHING THE FOLLIES AND VANITIES OF OUR YOUTH.

Alack, when I looke back
  Vpon my youth that's past,
And deepelie ponder youth's offense,
  And youth's reward at last;

With sighes and sobs I saie:—
  O God, I not denie
My youth with follie hath deseru'd
  With follie for to die.

But yet if euer sinfull man
  Might mercie mooue to ruth,
Good Lord, with mercie doo forgiue
  The follies of my youth.

In youth I rangde the fields,
  Where vices all do grow;
In youth I wanted grace
  Such vice to ouerthrow.

In youth what I thought sweet,
  Most bitter now I finde:
Thus hath the follies of my youth
  With follie kept me blinde.

Yet as the eagle casts hir bill,
  Whereby hir age renuth;
So, Lord, with mercie doo forgiue
  The follies of my youth.

A DIALOG BETWEENE CHRIST AND A SINNER.

Christ.

AWAKE from sleepe, and watch awhile,
  Prepare yourselues to praie;
For I mine angell will send foorth
  To sound the iudgement daie;
That mine elect and chosen sort
  Might find my saieng true,
How that the time I shorten will
  For them, and not for you.
  Awake, I saie, awake, awake.

Sinner.

And yet, O Lord, the little whelps
  Would like the crums that fall:
Thy chosen sort are verie few,
  But manie doost thou call.

Christ.

I call to you that will not heare,
  I stretch mine armes at large,
For to imbrace such as doo come,
  And all your sinnes discharge.
Wherefore if you refuse to come
  I will you then forsake,
And to my feast will strangers call,
  And them my children make.
Awake, therefore, and rise from sleepe;
  Awake, I saie, awake.

Sinner.
Not so, good Lord, thy mercie far
　Aboue our sinnes abound.

Christ.
And yet I will a iusticer
　In iustice mine be found.

Sinner.
Thy promise is to pardon sinne,
　And therein art thou iust.

Christ.
Your sinnes repent, and praie therefore ;
　In vaine is else your trust.

Sinner.
O Lord, thy grace must this performe,
　Or else it cannot be.

Christ.
My grace you haue, the same applie,
　And blessed shall you be.

Sinner.
Through this sweet grace thy mercie, Lord,
　We humblie doo require.

Christ.
By mercie mine I you forgiue,
　And grant this your desire.

A MEDITATION.

BEFORE thy face, and in thy sight
　Haue I, deuoid of shame,
O Lord, transgressed willinglie ;
　I doo confesse the same.

Yet was I loth that men should knowe,
  Or vnderstand my fall:
Thus feard I man much more than thee,
  Thou righteous Iudge of all.

So blind was I and ignorant—
  Yea, rather wilfull blind—
That suckt the combe, and knew the bee
  Had left hir sting behind.

My sinnes, O God, to thee are knowne,—
  There is no secret place,
Where I may hide myselfe or them
  From presence of thy face.

Where shall I then myselfe bestowe?
  Or who shall me defend?
None is so louing as my God—
  Thy mercies haue no end.

In deede, I grant, and doo confesse,
  My sinnes so hainous bee,
As mercie none at all deserues,—
  But yet thy propertie

Is alwaies to be mercifull
  To sinners in distresse;
Whereby thou wilt declare and shew
  Thy great Almightinesse.

Haue mercie, Lord, on me therefore
  For thy great mercies' sake,
Which camst not righteous men to call,
  But sinners' part to take.

AN HUMBLE SUTE OF A REPENTANT SINNER FOR MERCIE.

Giue eare, O Lord, to heare
  My heauie carefull cries;
And let my wofull plaints ascend
  Aboue the starrie skies.
And now receiue the soule
  That puts his trust in thee:
And mercie grant to purge my sinnes—
  Mercie, good Lord, mercie.

My soule desires to drinke
  From fountaine of thy grace;
To slake this thirst, O God, vouchsafe,
  And turne not of thy face:
But bow thy bending eare
  With mercie, when I crie,
And pardon grant for sinfull life—
  Mercie, good Lord, mercie.

Behold at length, O Lord,
  My sore repentant mind,
Which knocks with faith, and hopes thereby
  Thy mercies great to find.
Thy promise thus hath past,
  From which I will not flie:
Who dooth repent, trusting in thee,
  Shall taste of thy mercie.

A PSALME OF REIOISING FOR THE WOONDERFULL LOUE OF CHRIST,

RATIFIED BY HIS MERITORIOUS DEATH AND PASSION FOR OUR SPIRITUALL REDEMPTION.

Let vs be glad, and clap our hands,
  With ioie our soules to fill;

For Christ hath paid the price of sinne,
  With mercie and good will.
By his good will he flesh became
  For sinfull fleshe's sake;
By his good will disdained not
  Most shamefull death to take.
By his good will his blood was spilt,
  His bodie all-to rent;
By his good will to saue vs all
  He therewith was content.
By his good will death hath no power
  Our sinfull soules to kill;
For Christ hath paid the price of sinne
  With mercie and good will.
Since Christ so dearelie loued vs,
  Let us from sinne refraine;
For Christ desireth nothing els
  In lieu of all his paine:
And that we should each other loue,
  As he vs loou'd before;
So shall his loue abide in vs,
  And dwell for euermore.
Let then our loue so dwell in him,
  Our wicked lusts to kill:
For Christ hath paid the price of sinne
  With mercie and good will.

GRAY HEARES.

These heares of age are messengers,
Which bidde me fast, repent, and pray:
They be of death the harbingers,
That dooth prepare and dresse the way.
Wherefore I ioie that you may see
Upon my head such heares to be.

They be the lines that lead the length,
How farre my race is for to runne:
They say my youth is fled with strength,
And how olde age is weake begunne.
The which I feele, and you may see
Upon my head such lines to be.

They be the stringes of sober sound,
Whose musicke is harmonicall:
Their tunes declare a time from ground
I came, and how thereto I shall.
Wherefore I ioie that you may see
Upon my head such stringes to be.

God graunt to those that white heares haue
No worse them take then I haue ment:
That after they be layde in grauc,
Their soules may ioie their lives well spent.
God graunt likewise, that you may see
Upon your head such heares to be.

GOD'S COVENANT WITH NOAH.

To Noah and his sonnes with him
    God spake, and thus sayd he:—
A cou'nant set I vp with you
    And your posterity;

And with eche liuing creature els
    That from the flood was free,
Both foule and beast and cattel all,
    And what so ere it be,

Upon the earth that was with them,
    And from the arke did passe,
According eu'ry lyuing thinge,
    As then my pleasure was.

This is the cou'naunt that I make,
  From henceforth neuermore
Whill I agayne the worlde destroye
  With water, as before.

And of my cou'naunt this shall be
  The sygne and token sure,
Twene me and you and all the world
  For euer to indure.

My bowe in cloud I haue there set,
  That when a clowde shall falle,
This bowe therein shall then be seene
  Of liuing creatures all.

And I wil not vnmyndful be
  Of this my cou'naunt past
Twixt me and you and euery flesh,
  Whyles that the worlde shall last;

But stil will thinke vpon the same,
  And loke vpon the bowe,
The token, signe, and seale most sure
  Of couenaunt that I showe.

XIII.

THOMAS BRYCE.

THIS BOOKE TO THE READER.

Peruse with pacience, I thee praye,
My symple style, and metre base;
The works of God with wisdome waye,
The force of loue, the strength of grace.

Loue caused God his grace to giue
To such as shoulde for hym be slayne:
Grace wrougt in theym, while thei did liue,
For loue to loue their Christ agayne.

Now grace is of such strength and might,
That nothing may the same withstande:
Grace putteth death and hell to flight,
And guydes vs to the lyuing lande.

The force of loue also is suche,
That feare and payne it doeth expell:
Loue thynketh nothing ouermuche;
Loue doth all earthly thynges excell.

Thus loue and grace of God began
To worke in them to dooe hys wyll:
These, vertue's force, wrought loue in man,
That feare was past theyr bloude to spill.

THE REGESTER.
1555.
June.

When worthy Wattes with constant crie
Continued in the flamyng fier;
When Simson, Hawkes, and Jhon Ardite,
Did tast the tyrante's raging yre;
 When Chamberlaine was put to death,
 We wisht for our Elizabeth.

When blessed Butter and Osmande
With force of fyre to death were brent;
When Shitterdun, Sir Franke, and Blande,
And Humfrey Middleton of Kent;
 When Minge in Maistone toke his death,
 We wisht, etc.

July.

When Bradford, beautified with blisse,
When yong Jhon Least in Smithfield died;
When they like brethren both did kisse,
And in the fyre were truely tried;
 When teares were shed for Bradford's death,
 We wysht, etc.

When Dirick Harman lost his lyfe;
When Launder in their fume they fried;
When they sent Euerson from stryfe,
With moody mindes and puffed pride;
 When Wade at Dartford died the death,
 We wisht, etc.

When Richard Hooke, limlesse and lame,
At Chichester did beare the crosse;
When humble Hall for Christe's name
Ensued the same with worldly losse;
 When Jone Polley was brent to death,
 We wysht, etc.

When William Ailewarde at Redding
In prison died of sickenesse soore;
When Abbes, which fained a recanting,
Did wofully wepe and deplore;
  When he at Bery was done to death,
  We wishte, etc.

August.

When Denly died at Uxbridge towne,
With constant care to Christe's cause;
When Warren's widow yelded downe
Her flesh and bloud for holy lawes;
  When she at Stratforde died the death,
  We wishte, etc.

When Laurence, Collier, Coker, and Stere,
At Cantorbury were causeless slayne,
With Hopper and Wright, six in one fier,
Conuerted flesh to earth agayne;
  When Roger Corier was done to death,
  We wishte, etc.

When Tankerfield at St Albon's,
And William Bamford spent his bloud;
When harmefull hartes as hard as stones
Brent Robert Smith and Steuen Harwood;
  When Patrick Pattenham died the death,
  We wishte, etc.

When Jhon Newman and Thomas Fusse
At Ware and Walden made their ende;
When William Hailes for Christ Jesus
With breath and bloude did still contende;
  When he at Barnet was put to death,
  We wishte, etc.

When Samuell did firmely fight,
Till flesh and bloud to ashes went;

When constant Cob, with faith vpright,
At Thetforde cruelly was brent;
　When these with joy did take their death,
　We wishte, etc.

September.

When William Allen at Walsingham
For trueth was tried in fiery flame;
When Roger Cooe, that good olde man,
Did lose his lyfe for Christe's name;
　When these with other were put to death,
　We wishte, etc.

When Bradbridge, Streter, and Burwarde,
Tuttie, and George Painter of Hyde,
Vnto their duty had good regarde,
Wherefore in one fier they were fried;
　When these at Cantorbury toke their death,
　We wishte, etc.

When Jhon Lesse, prisoner in Newgate,
By sickenes turned to yerth and claye;
When wicked men, with yre and hate,
Brent Thomas Heywarde and Goreway;
　When Tingle in Newgate toke his death,
　We wishte, etc.

When Richard Smith in Lowlar's tower,
Androwes and Kyng, by sickenes died,
In faier fieldes they had their bower,
Where earth and clay doth still abide;
　When they in this wise did die the death,
　We wishte, etc.

When Glouer and Cornelius
Were fiercely brent at Couentrie;
When Wolsey and Pigot for Christ Jesus
At Ely felt like crueltie;
　When the pore bewept master Glouer's death,
　We wishte, etc.

October.

When learned Ridley and Latymer
Without regarde were swiftly slayne;
When furious foes could not confer
But with reuenge and mortall paine;
   When these two fathers were put to death,
   We wishte, etc.

When worthy Web and George Roper
In Elyes' chayre to heauen were sent;
Also, when Gregory Paynter
The same streight path and voiage went;
   When they at Cantorbury toke their deth,
   We wishte, etc.

December.

When godly Gore in pryson died,
And Wiseman in the Lowlar's towre;
When master Philpot, truely tryed,
Ended his life with peace and power;
   When he kissed the chayne at his death,
   We wishte, etc.

1556.
January.

When Thomas Whitwell and Bartlet Grene,
Annis Foster, Jone Lasheforde, and Browne,
Tutson and Winter, these seuen were sene
In Smithfield beate their enemies doune,
   Euen fleshe and deuil, world and death,
   Then we wishte for Elizabeth.

When Jhon Lowmas and An Albright,
Jone Soale, Jone Painter, and Annis Snod,
In fier with flesh and bloud did fight;
When tonges of tyrantes layed on lode;
   When these at ones were put to death,
   We wishte, etc.

February.

When two women in Ippeswiche towne
Joyfully did the fier embrace;
When they sange out with chereful sounde
Their fired foes for to deface;
    When Norwich Nobody[1] put them to deth,
    We wishte, etc.

March.

When constant Cranmer lost his life,
And helde his hande vnto the fier;
When streames of teares for him were rife,
And yet did misse their iust desier;
    When popysh power put him to death,
    We wishte, etc.

When Spencer and two brethren more
Were put to death at Salisbury;
Ashes to earth did right restore,
They being then ioyfull and mery;
    When these with violence were put to deth,
    We wyshte, etc.

Apryll.

When Hulliarde, a pastour pure,
At Cambridge did this life despise;
When Hartpoole's death thei did procure,
To make his flesh a sacrifice;
    When Jone Beche, widow, was done to deth,
    We wishte, etc.

When William Timmes, Ambrose, and Drake,
Spurge, Spurge, and Cauell, duely died,
Confessing that for Christe's sake
They were content thus to bee tried;

---

[1] Hopton, bishop of Norwich.

When London Little-grace[2] put them to death,
We wyshte, etc.

When lowly Lister, Nicol, and Mace,
Jhon Hammond, Spencer, and Yren also,
At Colchester, in the posterne place,
Joyfully to their death did go;
   When two at Glocester were put to death,
   We wishte, etc.

May.

When Margaret Eliot, being a maide,
After condemyning in prison died;
When lame Lauarocke the fire assaide,
And blinde Aprice with him was tryed;
   When these two impotentes were put to death,
   We wishte, etc.

When Katherine Hut did spend her bloude,
With two maides, Elizabeth and Jone;
When they embraste both rede and woode,
Trusting in Christ his death alone;
   When men vnnatural drew these to death,
   We wishte, etc.

When two men and a syster dere
At Bekelles were consumed to dust;
When William Sleeke, constant and cleare,
In prison died with hope and trust;
   When these our brethren wer put to death,
   We wyshte, etc.

June.

When John Oswold and Thomas Reede,
Harland, Milwright, and Euington,
With blasing brandes their bloude did bleede,
As their brethren before had done;

---

[2] Bonner, bishop of London.

When tyranny draue these to death,
We wishte, etc.

When Whod, the pastor, with Thomas Milles,
At Lewes lost this mortall gayne,
Compast with speares and bloudye bylles
Vnto the stake for to bee slayne;
   When William Adheral did die the death,
   We wishte, etc.

When Jackson, Holywel, and Wye,
Bowier, Laurence, and Addlington;
When Roth, Searles, Lion, and Hurst, did die,
With whom two women to death were done;
   When Dorifall with them was put to death,
   We wishte, etc.

When Thomas Parret, prisoner,
And Martyne Hunte died in the King's Bench,
When the yong man at Lecester
And Clemente died with filthie stenche;
   When Careless so toke his death,
   We wishte, etc.

July.

When Askue, Palmer, and Jhon Gwin,
Were brent with force at Newbury;
Lamenting onely for theyr sinne,
And in the Lorde were full mery:
   When tyrantes merciles put these to death,
   We wishte, etc.

When Jhon Foreman and mother Tree
At Grenstede cruelly were slaine;
When Thomas Dungate, to make vp three,
With them did passe from wo and payne;
   When these with other were put to death,
   We wishte, etc.

1557.

January.

When two at Asheforde with crueltie
For Christe's cause to death were brent;
When not long after two at Wye
Suffered for Christ his testament;
   When wyly wolues put these to death,
   We wishte, etc.

Apryll.

When Stanlye's wife and Annis Hide,
Sturtle, Ramsey, and Jhon Lothesby,
Were contente tormentes to abide,
And toke the same right paciently;
   When these in Smithfield wer done to death,
   We wisht, etc.

May.

When William Morant and Steuen Grathwick
Refusde with falshode to bee beguilde,
And for the same were burned quicke
With fury in St George's Fielde;
   When these with other were put to death,
   We wyshte, etc.

June.

When Jone Bradbridge, and a blind maide,
Appleby, Allen, and bothe their wiues;
When Manning's wife was not afrayde;
But al these seuen did lose their liues;
   When these at Maistone were put to death,
   We wishte, etc.

When Jhon Fiscoke, Perdue, and White,
Barbara, widow, and Bendens' wife,

With Wilson's wife, did firmly fight,
And for their faith al lost their life;
 When these at Cantorbury died the death,
 We wysht, etc.

When William Mainarde, his maide, and man,
Margery Mories and her sonne,
Dents, Burges, Steuens, and Wodman,
Gloue's wife and Ashdon's, to death were done;
 When one fyre at Lues brought to their death,
 We wishte, etc.

July.

When Ambrose died in Maistone gaile,
And so set free from tyrauntes' hands;
When Simon Milner they did assayle,
Hauing him and a woman in bandes;
 When these at Norwich were don to death,
 We wishte, etc.

When ten at Colchester in one daye
Were fried with fyre of tyrantes stoute;
Not once permitted trueth to say,
But were compast with billes aboute;
 When these with other were put to death,
 We wishte, etc.

When George Egles at Chelmsford towne
Was hanged, drawen, and quartered;
His quarters carried vp and doune,
And on a pole thei set his head;
 When wrested law put him to death,
 We wyshte, etc.

When Thurston's wife at Chichester,
And Bowmer's wife with her also;
When two women at Rochester,
With father Fruier, were sent from wo;

When one at Norwich did die the death,
We wyshte, etc

August.

When Joyce Bowes at Lichefield died,
Continuing constant in the fier;
When tired faith was truely tried,
Hauing her iuste and long desier;
  When she with others were put to death,
  We wishte, etc.

When Richard Rooth and Rafe Glaiton,
With James Auscoo and his wife,
Were brent with force at Islyngton,
Ending this short and sinneful life;
  When thei in cherefulnes did take their death,
  We wyshte, etc.

October.

When Sparrow, Gibson, and Hollingday,
In Smithfield did the stake embrace;
When fire conuerted fleshe to clay,
Thei being ioyfull of such grace;
  When lawless libertie put them to death,
  We wishte, etc.

December.

When Jhon Roughe, a minister weke,
And Margaret Mering, with corage died,
Because Christ onely they did seeke,
With fier of force they must bee fried;
  When these in Smithfield were put to death,
  We wishte, etc.

1558.

Marche.

When that Jhon Denneshe and Hugh Foxe
In Smithfielde cruell wrath sustained,

As fixed foes to Romish rockes,
And Cuthbert Symion, also Hayne;
   When these did worthely receyue their death,
   We wishte, etc.
When Dale disseast in Bery gaile,
According to God's ordinaunce;
When widow Thurstone thei did assaile,
And brought An Banger to death his daunce;
   When these at Colchester were done to death,
   We wishte, etc.

Apryll.

When William Nicoll in Harforwest
Was tryed with their fiery fan;
When Symon fought against the best,
With Glouer and Thomas Carman;
   When these at Norwiche did die the death,
   We wyshte, etc.

Maye.

When William Harris and Richard Day
And Christian George by them was brent,
Holding their enemies at baye,
Till life was lost and breath all spent;
   When these at Colchester wer put to death,
   We wyshte, etc.

June.

When Southam, Launder, and Ricarbie,
Hollyday, Holland, Houde, and Flood,
With cherefull look and constant crie,
For Christe's cause did spend their bloud;
   When these in Smithfield wer put to death,
   We wishte, etc.

When Thomas Tyler past this place,
And Matthew Withers also died;
Though sute were much, yet little grace
Among the rulers could be spied;

In prison paciently they tooke their death,
We wishynge for Elizabeth.

July.

When Richard Yeman, minister,
At Norwich did his life forsake;
When master Benbrike at Winchester
A liuely sacrifice did make;
   When these with other were put to death,
   We wishte, etc.

When William Peckes, Cotton, and Wreight,
The popish power did soore inuade,
To burning schole thei wer sent streight,
And with them went constant Jhon Slade;
   When these at Bramford wer put to death,
   We wishte, etc.

Nouember.

When Alexander Geche was brent,
And with him Elizabeth Launson;
When thei with ioye did both consent
To doe as their brethren had done;
   When these at Ipswich were put to death,
   We wishte, etc.

When Jhon Dauy, and eke his brother,
With Philip Humfrey, kist the crosse;
When they did comfort one another
Against all feare and worldlye losse;
   When these at Bery were put to death,
   We wishte, etc.

When laste of all, to take theyr leaue,
At Cantorbury they did consume,
Who constantly to Christ did cleaue,
Therefore were fried with fierie fume,—
   But sixe daies after these were put to death
   God sent vs our Elizabeth.

Our wished welth hath brought vs peace:
Our ioy is full, our hope obtayned;
The blasing brandes of fier doe cease,
The sleaying sworde also restrayned;
 The simple shepe preserued from death
 By our good queene Elizabeth.

As hope hath here obtained her pray,
By Godde's good will and prouidence;
So trust doth truely looke for staye
Through his heauenly influence,
 That great Golia shall be put to death
 By our good queene Elizabeth:

That Godde's trew word shall placed be,
The hungrie soules for to sustaine;
That perfite loue and vnitie
Shall be set in their seate agayne;
 That no more good men shal be put to death,
 Seeing God hath sent Elizabeth.

Pray we, therefore, both night and day,
For her highnes, as we bee bounde:
Oh Lorde, preserue this braunch of bay,
And all her foes with force confounde;
 Here long to lyue, and after death
 Receyue our queene Elizabeth.
        Amen.

Apoc. 6.

How long tariest thou, O Lorde, holy and trewe, to iudge and aduenge our blood on them that dwell on the earth?

THE WYSHES OF THE WISE.

The wishes of the wise,
Which longe to be at rest;
To God with lifted iyes
Thei call to be redreste.

WHEN shal this time of trauail cease,
  Which we with wo sustayne?
When shal the daies of rest and peace
  Returne to vs agayne?

When shall the minde be moued right
  To leaue hys lustyng life?
When shall our mocions and delight
  Be free from wrath and strife?

When shall the tyme of wofull teares
  Be moued vnto myrth?
When shall the aged with gray heares
  Reioyce at children's byrth?

When shall Hierusalem reioyce
  In him that is their Kyng,
And Sion hill with cherefull voyce
  Synge psalmes with triumphyng?

When shall the walles erected bee,
  That foes with furie fraye?
When shall that perfect oliue-tree
  Geue odour like the haye?

When shall the vineyard be restorde
  That beastlye bores deuour?
When shall the people, late abhorde,
  Receuye a quiet houre?

When shal the spirit more feruent be
  In vs that want good wyll?

When shall thy mercies set vs free
  From wickednesse and yll?

When shall the serpentes, that surmise
  To poyson thine electe,
Be bounde to better exercise,
  Or vtterly reiecte?

When shall the bloude reuenged be
  Which on the earth is shed?
When shall synne and iniquitie
  Be caste into the ded?

When shall that man of synne appeare
  To bee euen as he is?
When shal thy babes and children dere
  Receyue eternall blisse?

When shall that painted hore of Rome
  Be cast vnto the grounde?
When shal her children haue their dome,
  Which vertue would confounde?

When shall thy spouse and turtle-doue
  Be free from bitter blaste?
When shal thy grace our sinnes remoue
  With pardon at the laste?

When shal this lyfe translated bee
  From fortune's fickell fall?
When shall true faith and equitie
  Remaine in generall?

When shall contention and debate
  For euer slake and cease?
When shall the daies of euill date
  Be tourned vnto peace?

When shall trew dealing rule the roste
  With those that bye and sell,

THE WISHES OF THE WISE.

And single minde in euery coaste
    Among vs bide and dwell?

When shall our mindes wholly conuert
    From wealth and worldlye gayne?
When shall the monynges of our harte
    From wickednes refrayne?

When shall this flesh retourne to duste,
    From whence the same did spryng?
When shal the triall of our trust
    Appeare with triumphyng?

When shal the trumpe blow out his blast,
    And thy dere babes reuiue?
When shal the hoare be headlong cast,
    That sought vs to depryue?

When shall thy Christ our Kyng appeare
    With power and renowne?
When shall thy sainctes that suffer here
    Receyue their promest crowne?

When shall the faithfull firmely stande
    Before thy face to dwell?
When shall thy foes at thy lyfte hand
    Be caste into the hell?

XIV.

SIR NICHOLAS BRETON.

STANZAS

From "A small Handfull of Fragrant Flowers, gathered out of the Lovely Garden of Sacred Scriptures, fit for any honorable or worshippfull Gentlewomen to smell to."

DEARE dames, your sences to revive,
   Accept these flowers in order heare:
Then, for the time you are alive,
   Renowne your golden dayes shall beare.
Marke therefore what they have to name,
And learne to imitate the same.

The first resembleth Constancie,
   A worthie budde of passing fame;
Which every gentle certeinlie
   Delightes to chuse of, for the name.
The cause is, that, the truth to tell,
It sents and savours passing well.

*   *   *   *   *

This pleasaunt braunche in Sarae's brest
   Was dayly used for a showe;
So that her fayth among the rest
   Thereby did bountifullie growe:
And she extolled was therefore,
As noble matrone evermore.

*   *   *   *   *

The second budde is Modestie,
   Which Triata did much delight,

And furnished the companie
  Of many a Roman matrone bright;
So that no blemish there did growe,
As long as they the same could showe.

The third is vertuous Exercise;
  The fourth is called Humilitie;
The fifth, to set before your eyes
  The feare of God most reverently;
The sixth, obedience to the crowne,
And princes' lawes, with great renowne.

The seventh is Pacience, for to beare
  The crosse of Christe continually;
The eyght is liberall talke to heare,
  And use the same indifferently;
The ninth is called Chastitie;
The tenth to put up injurie.

The eleventh is, to sustayne the poore;
  The twelfth to aide the comfortlesse,
And to endeavour more and more
  To trayne your steppes to godlynes:
The thirtenth, that is cheefest skill,
Which we doo call—do good for ill.

The fourtenth is, to love the trouth,
  And flatterie wholy for to shunne;
The feftenth, barre the chaire of slouth,
  Whereby full many are undoune:
For idleness doth shame but wynne,
And is the entraunce unto sinne.

The sixtenth flower is willing zeale
  Unto the sacred veritie,
Which is a lanterne to your feete,
  To leade you to sinceritie:
The sevententh blossom fresh of hue,
In wordes and deedes for to be true.

The eyghtenth is, for to restore
    That by oppression hath ben gotte;
The niententh, for to cure that sore
    Which careless conscience makes to rotte:
The twenteth is sweet Charitie,
The fruites whereof begin to dye.

There are, besides these, godly love;
    Whose leaves though they be not so greene,
Yet who to plucke thereof wyl prove,
    Shall with Lucrecia soone be seene
To shine in wordes and deedes as bright
As when the moone doth yeelde her lyght.

Loe, gentles! this small bunch of Flowres
    It is that may encrease your fame;
For they be watered with the showres
    That Sacred Scriptures have to name:
You may discerne them by the seedes,
Full much vnlike to worldly weedes.

A PRAYER FOR GENTLEWOMEN AND OTHER TO USE,

Whereby, through the helpe of the devine grace, they may attayne the right sente of this Posie of Godly Flowres.

VOUCHSAFE, O Lord! to be our guide;
    The Spirit of grace into us powre!
Defende our cause on every side,
    That we may pass into the bowre,
Where as those heavenly flowres do growe
By Christ that garden first dyd sowe.

Illuminate our inwarde minde
    To seeke to Thee continually;
From worldly errours that be blind
    Preserve us for thy majestie.

Teach us, as we in wordes professe,
In deedes each one to do no lesse.

Assist us dayly to beginne
  Spiritually to enter fight
Agaynst the worlde, the flesh, and sinne;
  That we may shunne the duskie night,
In whiche our enemie, the devill,
Doth watche to worke each Christian evyll.

Arm us with fayth, to beare the shielde,
  And sworde of heavenlie puritie;
Crowne us with helmet in the fielde
  Of thy surpassing veritie.
Graunt this, O bounteous Jesu sweete,
That we with Thee at last may meete.

A SOLEMPNE AND REPENTANT PRAYER FOR FORMER LIFE MISPENT.

Oh heavenly Lord! who plain doost see
  The thoughts of ech man's heart;
Who sendest some continuall plague,
  And some relief of smart;

Pittie, O Lorde! the wofull state
  Wherein I dayly stand;
And onely for thy mercies' sake
  Now helpe me out of hande.

And as it was thy pleasure fyrst,
  To plague me thus with greefe;
So canst thou, Lorde, if thee it please,
  With speede send me releefe.

I must of force confesse, O Lorde!
  I can it not denye,
That I deserve these plagues, and worse,
  And that continually.

Yet doo not Thou therefore on me
  Thy judgments just extend;
But pardon me, and graunt me grace
  My life for to amend.

And banish, Lord! from me delights
  Of worldly vanitie,
And lend me helpe to pace the pathes
  Of perfect pietie;

And truly so to tread the pathes,
  And in such godly wise,
That they may bring me to the place
  Of perfect Paradice.

And not to wander up and downe
  In wayes of weary wo,
Where wicked, wily, wanton toyes
  Do leade me too and fro.

The sap of Sapience likes me not,
  That pleaseth not my taste;
But fond delight, that wicked weede,
  Was all my chief repaste:

Wherein, as hooke within the baight,
  So doo I plainly finde
Some hidden poyson lurking lyes
  For to infect my minde.

But wherefore doo I finde it now?
  Because I now do see
That, wanting smart, I wanted grace
  For to acknowledge thee.

But now, O Lord, that I so sore
  Doo feele thy punishment,
I doo lament my folly great,
  And all my sinnes repent.

A SOLEMN AND REPENTANT PRAYER.

And to thy heavenly throane, O Lord!
  For mercy I appeale,
To send me, Lord, some heavenly salve
  My greevous sores to heale.

Beholde, O Lord! my sorrowes such
  As no man dooth endure;
And eke my greevous sicknesse such
  As none but Thou canst cure.

And as thou art a gratious God
  To men in misery,
So pitty me, that thus, O Lord!
  Do pine in penurie.

And as Thou art a help to all
  That put their trust in Thee,
So held in this my deepe distresse
  Some comfort lend to me.

And hold, O Lord! thy heavy hand,
  And lay thy scourge aside;
For, Lord, the greevous smart thereof
  I can no longer bide.

Forgive my sinnes, forget the same;
  Beholde my humble heart,
Who onely, Lord, doo trust in thee
  For to releeve my smart.

And after this my wretched life,
  Lord, graunt me of thy grace,
That I in heauen at latter daye
  May have a joyfull place.

A PRAYER.

Plante, Lorde, in me the tree of godly lyfe;
  Hedge me about with the strong fence of faith:
If thee it please, use eke thy proyning knife,
  Least that, oh Lord! as a good gardiner saith,
    If suckers draw the sappe from roots on hie,
    Perhaps, in tyme, the top of tree may die.
Let, Lord, this tree be set within thy garden-wall
Of Paradise, where growes no one ill sprigg at all.

A PRAYER WRITTEN FOR A GENTLE-WOMAN.

Pitie, oh Lord, thy seruaunt's heavy heart;
  Her sinnes forgiue, that thus for mercy cryes:
Judge no man, Lorde, according to desart;
  Let fall on her with speede thy healthfull eyes,
    In hart who prayes to thee continually,
    Putting her only trust, O[1] God, in Thee!
Lorde! Lorde! to Thee for mercy still I call:
O set me free, that thus am bound and thrall.

THE PRAYSE OF HUMILITIE.

Oh, the sweete sence of loue's humilitie,
Which feares displeasure in a deerest friend;
The only note of true nobilitie,
Whose worthy grace is graced without end;
While faythfull loue, in humble truth approued,
Doth euer liue, of God and man beloued.

Her grace is gratious in the sight of God;
Makes men as saincts, and women angells seeme;
Makes sinne forgotten; mercy vse no rodd;
And constant fayth to growe in great esteeme;

---

[1] Old edition, *of*.

And is, in summe, a blessing of the highest,
And to the nature of himselfe the nighest.

It maketh beawty like the sunne to shine,
As if on earth there were a heau'nly light:
It maketh witt in wisedome so diuine,
As if the eie had a celestiall sight:
It is a guide vnto that heauen of rest,
Where blessed soules doe liue for euer blest.

In Christ it is a grace of worthy glory;
In man, from God a guift of speciall grace;
While in the state of vertues, honor's story,
Wisedome doth find itt in perfection's place;
And plac't so high in the Allmightie's loue,
As nothing more can mercie's comfort proue.

It makes the eie looke down into the harte;
The harte obedient vnto witt and sence;
And euery limme to play a seruant's parte,
Vnto the will of witt's præheminence:
It brings the minde vnto the body soe,
That one the other cannott ouergoe.

It is the death of pride, and patience loue;
Passion's phisition; reason's councellour;
Religion's darling; labour's turtle-doue;
Learning's instructer; grace's register;
Time's best attendant, and truthe's best explainer;
Vertue's best louer, and loue's truest gainer.

It is the prince's grace; the subiect's duety;
The scholar's lesson, and the soldier's line;
The courtier's creditt, and the ladies' beawty;
The lawier's vertue; and the loue diuine,
That makes all sences gratious in his sight,
Where all true graces haue theyr glorious light.

Itt makes the harte fitt for all good impression;
Itt doth prepare the spirit for perfection;

Itt brings the sowle vnto her sinnes' confession;
Itt helpes to cleere the body from infection:
Itt is the meane to bring the minde to rest,
Where harte, sowle, body, minde, and all, are blest.

Itt made the mother of the Soonne of God
Gratious in him, who made her full of grace;
And on her Sonne itt blessedly abode,
In bearing all the filthy world's deface;
And in his seruants, for theyr Master's loue,
Did fayth's affections in theyr passions proue.

It saued Abraham's sonne from sacrifice,
When Isaack's death was quitted by the rame;
Itt saued Noah and his progenies,
When on the earth destruction's deluge came;
Itt saued Lott from hurt of Sodom's fire,
And Israell from cruel Pharaoh's ire.

Itt wrought in Dauid gratious penitence;
In Niniuie a sweete submission;
In Job a famous blessed patience;
In Pawle assurance of his sinnes' remission;
In John the habitt of a holy loue;
In Christ the grace that did all glory proue.

Itt euer holds the hand of faythfulnes;
And ever keeps the minde of godlynes;
And euer brings the harte to quietnes;
And euer leads the soule to happines;
And is a vertue of that blessednes,
That merits praise in highest worthines.

Oh, how it gaynes the child the parent's loue,
The wife her husband's, and the seruants master's;
Where humble fayth in happie hope's behoue
Finds patience, care discomfort's healing plasters,
And truest course of care's tranquilitie
Only to rest butt in humility.

And since that in the life of humble loue
I see the waye vnto the well of blisse,
Where patience doth in all perfection proue,
Where the high blessing of all blessing is;
Let my sowle pray that I may humbly sing
The heauenly prayses of my holy Kinge.

GLORIA IN EXCELSIS DEO.

O HOLY essence of all holynes;
Grace of all glory; glory of all grace;
Perfection's vertue; vertue's perfectnes;
Place of all beawtie; beawtie of all place;
Truthe's only tryall; tyme's æternitie;
Incomprehensible in thy Deitie:

Wisdome's deuiser; father of her loue;
Constancie's proofe, and life of patience;
Humilitie's essence; fayth's true turtle-doue;
Mercie's almighty glorious residence:
Sweete Jesus Christ, mine humble sowle en-
    flame,
To sing the glory of thy holy name.

Before what was, but that which euer is,
The Godhead, all incomprehensible;
Sweete Jesus Christ, the essence of all blisse,
But in his manhood only sensible,
My Sauiour was, and in himselfe alone
Contayning all things, but contaynd in none.

The nature of all vertues in his nature
Had all theyr essence of theyr only being,
When in creation of each kinde of creature
Wisdome in him had only all her seeing,
Whose loue in him yet constant patience found,
That of her grace and glory was the grownd.

His spotless vertue all his life did prove,
In doing good to all, and ill to none;
His wisedome did the doctors' wonder moue;
His loue the touchstone of all truth alone;
His constancie euen to his dying hower
Did shew his patience had a heauenly power.

And for the note of his humilitie
His crosse bare witness in his lyfe and death,
Who bare all basenes' inciuilitie,
Yitt neuer breath'd the smallest angry breath:
O glorious King, that came from heauen on high,
Vpon this earth for beggars so to dye.

His vertue in his will his woorde doth showe;
His wisedome in election and creation;
His loue his louers by his death do knowe;
His constancy his patience confirmation;
His patience his humilitie did proue;
And all, in summe, his glory from aboue.

Whose vertue such as his that could not sinne?
Whose wisdome such as woorketh vertues' witt?
Whose loue is such as wisedome liueth in?
Whose constancy doth shew such kindnes still?
Whose patience such as did his passion showe?
Or who so high and euer brought so low?

What vertue doth, his wisedome doth express;
What wisedome doth, his loue doth manifest;
What loue doth, doth his constancy confesse;
What constancy doth, in his patience blest;
What patience doth, humilitie doth tell;
In him alone they all and only dwell.

Then lett the vertuous for all vertue loue him;
And lett the wise in wisedome's loue admire him;
And let the constant in all kindenes proue him;
And lett the patient patiently desire him;

GLORIA IN EXCELSIS DEO.

And lett the humble humbly fall before him;
And all together all in all adore him.

Oh that the world could see his vertues' beawty;
Or witt of man his wisedome's maiestie;
Or loue could looke into his constancy;
Or patience into his humilitie!
Then vice, nor folly, frailtie, rage, nor pride,
Should in the minds of men so much abide.

His vertue made the first perfection's nature;
His wisedome made the forme of all perfection;
His loue did giue the lyfe to euery creature;
His constancy the care of loue's direction;
His patience medicine for all miseries,
His humblenes the waye to Paradice.

Wouldst thow be perfect? in his vertues knowe itt;
Wouldst thow be vertuous? in his wisedome learne
    itt;
Wouldst thow be wise? in his loue only show itt;
Wouldst thow be louing? in his life discerne itt;
Wouldst thow be constant? in his care conceiue itt;
Wouldst thow be patient? in his death perceiue itt.

Wouldst thow be humble? in his lowliness
Learne to submitt thyself to higher powers.
Wouldst thow be blessed? in his blessednes
Learne to bestow the labour of thine howers.
Wouldst thow be holy, and liue happie euer?
Liue in his loue, and thow shalt liue for euer.

The infinite good thoughts his vertue giueth,
The infinite good woorks his will perfecteth,
The infinite good lyfe in his loue liueth,
The infinite loue his constancie effecteth,
The infinite constancy his patience proueth,
Doe humblie shew with infinitenes loueth.

Since vertues, then, good thoughts are infinite,
And infinite in vertue is good thought;
And infinite in wisedome is good witt;
And infinite is loue by wisedome wrought;
And infinite is constancy in loue,
Which infinitely patience doth prooue:

In infinite humilitie of harte,
Vnto the height of all infinitie,
In infinite perfection of each parte
That makes the infinite Diuinitie;
The Father, Soonne, and Holy Ghost, all three
In one, one God, all infinite glory bee.

And since no harte is able to attayne
Vnto his holy and æternall praise,
To whom alone doth duly appertayne
The date of glories' neuer-ending dayes;
When angells in theyr halleluiah dwell,
Lett me but sing Amen, and I am well.

STANZAS

From "An Excellent Poeme upon the longing of a blessed heart, which loathing the world doth long to be with Christ."

MEN talke of loue that know not what it is;
For could we know what loue may be indeede,
We would not haue our mindes so led amisse
With idle toyes that wanton humours feede:
But in the rules of higher reason read
   What loue may be so from the world conceal'd,
   Yet all too plainely to the world reveal'd.

It is too cleare a brightnesse for man's eye;
Too high a wisedome for his wits to finde;

Too deepe a secret for his sense to trie;
And all too heauenly for his earthly minde:
It is a grace of such a glorious kinde
    As giues the soule a secret power to know it,
    But giues no heart nor spirit power to show it.

It is of heauen and earth the highest beautie;
The powerfull hand of heauen's and earth's crea-
    tion;
The due commander of all spirits' duetie;
The Deitie of angels' adoration;
The glorious substance of the soule's saluation:
    The light of truthe that all perfection trieth,
    And life that giues the life that neuer dieth.

It is the height of God, and hate of ill,
Tryumph of trueth, and falshood's ouerthrow;
The onely worker of the highest will,
And onely knowledge that doeth knowledge know,
And onely ground where it doeth onely growe:
    It is in summe the substance of all blisse,
    Without whose blessing all thing nothing is.

But in itselfe itselfe it all containeth,
And from itselfe but of itselfe it giueth;
It nothing loseth, and it nothing gaineth,
But in the glorie of itselfe it liueth,
A ioy which soone away all sorrow driueth:
    The prooued truth of all perfections' storie,
    Our God incomprehensible in glorie.

Thus is it not a riddle to be read,
And yet a secret to be found in reading;
But when the heart ioynes issue with the head,
In settled faith to seeke the Spirit's feeding,
While in the woundes, that euer fresh are bleeding
    In Christ his side, the faithfull soule may see
    In perfect life what perfect loue may be.

No further seeke then for to finde out loue
Than in the lines of euerliuing blisse,
Where carefull conscience may in comfort prooue
In sacred loue that heauenly substance is,
That neuer guides the gracious minde amisse;
    But makes the soule to finde in life's behoue
    What thing indeed, and nothing else, is loue.

Then make no doubt if either good or bad,
If this or that, in substance or in thought,
And by what meanes it may be sought or had,
Whereof it is, and how it may be wrought:
Let it suffice the word of truth hath taught:
    It is the grace but of the liuing God,
    Before beginning that with him abode.

It brought forth power to worke, wisdome to will,
Justice to iudge, mercie to execute,
Vertue to plant, charitie to fill,
Time to direct, truths falshood to confute,
Pitie to pleade in penitence's suite,
    Patience to bide, and peace to giue thee rest,
    To prooue how loue doth make the spirit blest.

And this is God, and this same God is loue,
For God and loue in Charitie are one:
And Charitie is that same God aboue,
In whome doth liue that onely loue alone,
Without whose grace true loue is neuer none:
    Then seeke no further what is loue to finde,
    But onely carie God within thy minde.

Leaue in the world to looke for any loue;
For on the earth is little faith to finde,
And faithlesse hearts in too much trueth doe proue
Loue doth not liue where care is so vnkind:
Men in their natures differ from their kinde:
    Sinne fils the world so full of secret euils,
    Men should be gods to men, but they are deuils.

STANZAS.

Christ lou'd to death, yet loue did neuer die;
For loue by death did worke the death of
    death!
Oh liuing loue! oh heauenly mysterie!
Too great a glory for this world beneathe,
The blessed breathing of the highest breathe.
   Blest are they borne that onely finde in thee,
   Oh blessed God, what blessed loue may be!

   *   *   *   *   *   *

Amidde the skie there is one onely sunne;
Amidde the ayre one onely phœnix flies;
One onely time by which all houres doe runne;
One onely life that liues and neuer dies;
One onely eye that euerie thought descries;
   One onely light that shewes our onely loue;
   One onely loue; and that is God aboue.

To say yet further what this loue may be,
It is a holy heauenly excellence;
Aboue the power of any eye to see,
Or wit to finde by world's experience:
It is the spirit of life's quintessence;
   Whose rare effects may partly be perceiued,
   But to the full can neuer be conceiued.

It is repentance' sweet restoratiue;
The *Rosa solis* the sicke soule reuiueth;
It is the faithfull heart's preseruatiue;
It is the hauen where happie grace arriueth;
It is the life that death of power depriueth:
   It is, in summe, the euerlasting blisse,
   Where God alone in all his glorie is.

It is a ioy that neuer comes in iest;
A comfort that doth cast off euery care;
A rule wherein the life of life doth rest,
Where all the faithfull finde their happie fare;
A good that doth but onely God declare;

A line that his right hand doth draw so euen,
As leads the soule the hyway unto heauen.

If then henceforth you aske what thing is loue,
In light, in life, in grace, in God, goe looke it;
And if in these you doe not truely prooue
How in your hearts you may for euer booke it,
Vnhappy thinke yourselues you haue mistook it:
  For why? the life that death hath ouer-trod
  Is but the loue of Grace, and that is God.

HYMNE.

When the angels all are singing
All of glorie euer springing
In the ground of high heauen's graces,
Where all vertues haue their places;
  Oh that my poore soule were neare them,
  With an humble heart to heare them!

Then should faith, in loue's submission
Ioying but in mercie's blessing,
Where that sinnes are in remission,
Sing the ioyful soule's confessing;
  Of her comforts high commending
  All in glorie neuer ending.

But, ah wretched sinfull creature!
How should the corrupted nature
Of this wicked heart of mine
Thinke vpon that loue diuine,
  That doth tune the angels' voices,
  While the hoast of heauen reioyces?

No! the songe of deadly sorrowe
In the night that hath no morrow,

And their paines are neuer ended
That haue heauenly powers offended,
  Is more fitting to the merite
  Of my foule infected spirit.

Yet while mercie is remoouing
All the sorrowes of the louing,
How can faith be full of blindnesse
To despaire of mercie's kindnesse;
  While the hand of heauen is giuing
  Comfort from the euer-liuing?

No, my soule, be no more sorie;
Looke vnto that life of glorie
Which the grace of faith regardeth,
And the teares of loue rewardeth;
  Where the soule the comfort getteth,
  That the angels' musique setteth.

There when thou art well conducted,
And by heauenly grace instructed
How the faithfull thoughts to fashion
Of a rauisht louer's passion,
  Sing with sainctes to angels nighest
  Halleluiah in the highest.
Gloria in excelsis Deo.

SONNETS

From "The Soules Harmony."

LORD, when I thinke how I offend thy will,
And know what good is in obedience to it,
And see my hurt, and yet continue still
In doing ill, and cannot leaue to do it;
And then againe doe feele that bitter smart
That inward breeds of pleasures after-paine,
When scarce the thought is entred in my heart

But it is gone, and sinne gets in againe:
And when againe the act of sinne is past,
And that thy grace doth call me backe againe,
Then in my teares I runne to thee as fast,
And of my sinnes and of myselfe complayne:
    What can I doe but cry, Sweet Iesus, saue me?
    For I am nothing but what thou wilt haue me.

My heauenly Loue, from that high throne of thine,
Where gracious mercy sits in glorie's seat,
In that true pity of thy power diuine,
That dries the teares that mercy doe entreat,
Behold, sweet Lord, these bleeding drops of loue
That melt my soule in sorrow of my sinne;
And let these showres some drops of mercy moue,
That in my griefe my comfort may beginne:
Let not despaire confound my praying hope,
That begs an almes at thy mercie's gate;
But let thy grace thy hand of bountie ope,
That comfort yeelds which neuer comes too late:
    That in the cure of my consuming griefe
    My ioyful soule may sing of thy reliefe.

XV.

JOHN HALL, M.D.

AN EXAMPLE OF PRAIER AGAINST IDOLATROUS TYRANTES,

THAT SET VP FALSE WORSHIP IN THE REPROCHE OF GOD'S TRUE WORSHYP.

Out of the cxv. *Psalme.*

If vnto vs poore mortall men
No prayse is due of very ryght,
How are they mockte and blynded then,
How farre are they from perfect sight,

That to a stocke or dead image
Will geue such laude as God should haue!
How vayne is he, howe doth he rage,
That doth God's glorie so depraue!

The which sinne and most vyle offence
David did so abhorre and hate,
That he a psalme in God's defence
Compiled hath, that each estate

May vnderstande howe farre awrye
They wandred be from righteousnes,
The lyuing God that doe denye
By an image or false lykenes:

And therfore doth all men exhorte
To feare the Lorde, and in hym truste;
Which is a true and sure comforte
To all that in his hope are iust.

His harpe in hande he therfore tooke,
And on his knees this noble kyng
(As it is in the Psalter booke)
This holy psalme begun to synge:

  Not vnto vs, Lord, not to vs,
                       Etc. etc. etc. etc.

PSALM CXV.

Non nobis, Domine.

Not unto us, Lord, not to us,
But to thy holy name alwayse,
For thy mercy and truthe done thus,
Ascribed be all laude and prayse.

These heathen folke that faythles be,
Why should they saye to us in spighte,
Where is their God, let us hym see,
In whom these Christians haue delyghte?

For their false gods, their chiefe and best,
Are nothing but syluer and goulde:
The handes of men, both most and lest,
Haue forged them out of the moulde.

Yet haue they for their idols made
Mouthes wherewith they can speak nothing,
And eyes also whereof the trade
Is to be blynde from all seyng.

Suche eares also in them are wrought,
And heare nothing that one can tell;
And noses whiche are likewyse nought,
For they with them can nothyng smell.

Vayne handes haue they, and fete also;
For with their handes they handle not,
Nor with their fete they can not goe,
Nor sounde no voice out of their throte.

Wherefore suche as doe idols make,
Doe their own works resemble just;
And they also that doe them take
For gods, or haue them in their truste.

Let Israell, then, in the Lorde
Set all their truste and confidence;
And Aaron's house thereto accorde;
For he is their most sure defence.

All ye that feare the Lorde aright,
Trust in hym well, be not afrayde;
For he will surely shewe his myght
To succoure you and be your ayde.

The Lord will not forget doubtless,
But haue us in his mynde full well:
The righteous houses he wyll bles
Of Aaron and of Israell.

Ye that do feare the Lorde therefore
Are blessed, both the great and small:
The Lorde increase you more and more,
Both you and eke your children all.

For sithe ye are his chosen sorte,
And haue the Lorde whole in your thought,
He wyll you blesse with greate comforte,
Both heauen and earth that made of nought.

The heauens and the firmament
Are his, and at his holy wyll;
But the rounde earth he hath forth lente
The sonnes of mortal men untyll[1].

The dead, O Lorde, that are gone hence,
Cannot in graue express thy wayes;
Nor such as downe are in sylence
Can honor thee or giue thee prayse.

---

[1] unto.

But we, O Lorde, that be alyve,
  Thy prayse wyll spreade and ramifye,
And in our hearts due thankes contryve
  Unto thy name eternally.

AN HOLSOME WARNING

FOR ALL MEN THAT BEARE THE NAME OF CHRISTIANS
TO LYVE CHRISTIANLY.

From the " Court of Vertue."

O HARKE a whyle vnto my style,
  All ye that Christians be;
That beare that name, and doe not frame
  Your liues accordingly.

Is fayth in syche as beying ryche,
  Though thee doo Christ professe,
That euery houre doo Christ deuoure,
  And his poore flocke oppresse?

For we are all, as sayth Saynt Paule,
  Membres of one body
Of Christ Jesu, ground of vertue
  And of all veritie:

When the poore man, as proue I can,
  Is Christ his member true,
As well as he, what so he be,
  That ryches so endue.

Why should ye then to symple men
  Beare such despight and hate,
Syth they be all in Christ equall
  With you in all estate?

Christ his kyngdome was neuer wonne
  By wealth or hygh degree,
Allthough that here some doo appere
  To reygne in dignitie.

AN WHOLESOME WARNING.

Then let none thynke that Christ wyll shrynke,
   When he shall iudge us all,
Of all your wealth, so got by stelthe,
   You to accompt to call:

When yf he fynde ye were unkynde
   To your poore brethern dere,
Then wyll he say, Goo from me aye
   Into eternall fyre.

When I lackt meate, and fayne would eate,
   In sycknes, thyrst, and colde,
In all my nede not one good dede
   That you to me doo wold.

Then wyll ye say wythout delay,
   Lord, when dyd we thee see
Lacke any foode to doo thee good,
   And dyd it not to thee?

And he agayne shall answer playne,
   I truely say to you,
Ye styll oppreste and muche detest
   The poore, my members true.

When ye therfore did them abhorre
   That are of lowe degree,
To me alone, and other none,
   Ye did that iniury.

Saint John doth proue we cannot loue
   God whom we doe not see,
If we doe hate our brethren that
   Are present to our eye.

Nowe call for grace, whyle ye haue space;
   Your wycked lyues amende;
And so procede in worde and dede
   True Christians to the ende.

THE FAITHFULL SOULDIOUR OF CHRISTE DESIRETH ASSISTANCE OF GOD AGAINST HIS GHOSTLY ENEMIES.

Hereout, O Lorde, the right request
Of him, that faine would haue redrest
The wronges that are so sore increst
Within my soule, so sore opprest.

O Lorde, to thee with wofull crye
I call for grace and for mercy;
And if thou helpe not then truly,
In deadly wo remayn must I.

The world, the diuell, death, and hell,
With great assaultes against me swell:
Lorde, let thy grace in me excell
Against their fury fierce and fell.

O Lorde my God, to thee I praye,
Suffer me not to goe astraye,
And haue in mynde the pryce and day
Wherewith thou didste my ransome pay.

Oh haue in mynde thine own great cost,
And let not this thy payne be lost:
In thee, O Lorde, my trust is most
To dwell among thy holy host.

Thou knowst wherin my help doth stand,
Whereuer I be on sea or lande:
Good Lorde, put to thy helping hand,
Saue me from hell, that fierce fyrebrand.

XVI.

GEFFREY WHITNEY.

EMBLEME I.

Motto: *Te stante virebo.*

A MIGHTIE spyre, whose toppe dothe pierce the skie,
An iuie greene imbraceth rounde about;
And while it standes, the same doth bloom on highe,
But when it shrinkes, the iuie standes in dowt.
  The piller great our gratious princes is;
  The braunche the churche, whoe speakes vnto hir this:

"I that of late with stormes was almoste spent,
And brused sore with tirants' bluddie bloes,
Whome fire and sworde with persecution rent,
Am nowe sett free, and ouerlooke my foes;
  And whiles thou raignst, oh most renowmed queene!
  By thie supporte my blossome shall be greene."

EMBLEME II.

Motto: *Veritas temporis filia.*

THREE furies fell, which turne the world to ruthe,
Both Enuie, Strife, and Slaunder, heare appeare:
In dungeon darke they longe inclosed Truthe;
But Time at lengthe did loose his daughter deare,
  And setts alofte that sacred ladie brighte,
  Which things longe hidd reueales and bringes to lighte.

Thoughe Strife make fier, thoughe Enuie eate
    hir harte,
The innocent though Slaunder rente and spoile;
Yet Time will comme, and take this ladie's parte,
And breake her bandes, and bring her foes to
    foile.
  Dispaire not then, thoughe Truthe be hidden
    ofte,
  Bycause at lengthe shee shall bee sett alofte.

EMBLEME III.

Motto: *Non tibi, sed religioni.*

THE pastors good, that doe gladd tidinges preache,
The godlie sorte with reuerence doo imbrace:
Though they be men, yet since Godd's worde they
    teache,
Wee honor them, and giue them higheste place:
  Imbassadors of princes of the earthe
  Haue royall seates, thoughe base they are by
    birthe.

Yet if throwghe pride they doe themselves forgett,
And make accompte that honor to be theires,
And doe not marke within whose place they sett,
Let them behowlde the asse that Isis beares,
  Whoe thowghte the men to honor him did
    kneele,
  And staied therfore till he the staffe did feele.

For as he passd with Isis throughe the streete,
And bare on backe his holie rites about,
The Ægyptians downe fell prostrate at his feete,
Whereat the asse grew arrogante and stowte:
  Then saide the guide, Oh foole! not vnto thee
  Theise people bowe, but vnto that they see.

EMBLEME IV.

Motto: *Qua dij vocant, eundum.*

THE trauaylinge man vncertain where to goe
When diuers wayes before his face did lie,
Mercurius then the perfect pathe did showe;
Which when he tooke, hee neuer went awrie,
    But to his wishe his iorney's ende did gaine,
    In happie howre, by his direction plaine.

This trauailinge man doth tell our wandringe state,
Before whose face and eeke on euerye side,
By-pathes and wayes appeare amidd our gate,
That if the Lorde be not our onlie guide,
    We stumble, fall, and dailie goe astraye:
    Then happie those whome God doth shew the waye.

EMBLEME V.

Motto: *Prouidentia.*

SVCHE prouidence hath nature secret wroughte
In creatures wilde, and eeke such knowledge straunge,
That man by them in somme thinges maie be taughte:
As some foretell when weather faire will chaunge;
    Of heate, of raine, of winde, and tempests' rage,
    Some showe by signes, and with their songs presage.

But leauing theise, which almost all doe knowe;
The crocodile, by whome th' Ægyptians watche'
Howe farre that yeare shall mightie Nilus flowe,
For theire shee likes to laie her egges and hatche:
    Such skill deuine, and science to foretell,
    Hath nature lente vnto this serpent fell.

Which showes they should with due regarde
  foresee,
When anie one doth take in hande a cause,
The drifte and ende of that they doe decree,
And longe thereon to ponder and to pause :
  For after-witts are like a shower of rayne,
  Which moistes the soile when witherd is the
    graine.

EMBLEME VI.

Motto: *Constanter.*

THE raging sea, that roares with fearefull sounde,
And threatneth all the world to ouerflowe,
The shore sometimes his billows doth rebounde,
Though oft it winnes, and giues the earthe a
  blowe :
  Sometimes where shippes did saile, it makes a
    lande ;
  Sometimes again they saile where townes did
    stande.

So if the Lorde did not his rage restraine,
And set his boundes so that it cannot passe,
The worlde should faile, and man could not remaine,
But all that is shoulde soone be turn'd to was.
  By raging Sea is ment our ghostlie foe ;
  By Earthe, man's soule he seekes to ouerthrowe.

And as the surge doth worke both daie and nighte,
And shakes the shore, and ragged rockes doth
  rente ;
So Sathan stirres with all his maine and mighte
Continuall siege our soules to circumuente :
  Then watche and praie for feare we sleepe in
    sinne ;
  For cease our crime, and hee can nothing winne.

EMBLEME VII.

Motto: *Veritas invicta.*

THOUGHE Sathan striue with all his maine and mighte
To hide the truthe, and dimme the lawe deuine;
Yet to his worde the Lorde doth giue such lighte,
That to the East and West the same doth shine:
  And those that are so happie for to looke,
  Saluation finde within that blessed booke.

EMBLEME VIII.

Motto: *Omnis caro fœnum.*

ALL fleshe is grasse, and witherth like the haie:
To-daie man laughes, to-morrowe lies in claie.
Then let him marke the frailtie of his kinde,
For here his tearme is like a puffe of winde;
Like bubbles smalle that on the waters rise;
Or like the flowers whom Flora freshlie dies,
Yet in one daie their glorie all is gone;
So worldlie pompe which here we gaze vppon:
Which warneth all that here their pageantes plaie,
Howe well to liue, but not how long to waie.

EMBLEME IX.

Motto: *Sic probantur.* Matt. xxiv.

THROUGHE tormentes straunge and persecutions dire
The Christians passe with pacience in their paine,
And ende their course sometime with sworde and fire,
And constant stand, and like to lambes are slaine:
  Bycause, when all their martirdome is past,
  They hope to gaine a glorious crowne at last.

EMBLEME X.

Motto: *Soli Deo Gloria.*

Here man with axe doth cut the bough in twaine,
And without him the axe could nothing doe;
Within the toole there doth no force remaine,
But man it is that mighte doth put thereto:
  Like to this axe is man in all his deedes,
  Who hath no strength but what from God proceedes.

Then let him not make vaunt of his desert,
Nor bragge thereof when he good deedes hath done;
For it is God that worketh in his harte,
And with his grace to good doth make him ronne.
  And of himselfe hee weake theretoo doth liue,
  And God giues power, to whom all glorie giue.

EMBLEME XI.

Motto: *Nemo potest duobus dominis seruire.*

Here man, who first should heauenlie thinges attaine,
And then to world his sences should incline,
First vndergoes the worlde with might and maine,
And then at foote doth drawe the lawes deuine:
  Thus God hee beares and Mammon in his minde,
  But Mammon first, and God doth come behinde.

Oh worldlinges fonde, that ioyne these two so ill,
The league is nought, throwe doune the world with speede:
Take vp the lawe, according to his will;
First seeke for heauen, and then for worldly neede:

But those that first their worldlie wishe doe serue,
Their gaine is losse, and seeke their soules to sterue.

EMBLEME XII.

Motto: *Superest quod supra est.*

ADVE, deceiptfull worlde, thy pleasures I detest;
Nowe others with thy showes delude; my hope in heauen doth rest.

Inlarged as followeth.

Even as a flower, or like vnto the grasse,
Which now dothe stande, and straight with sithe dotho fall[1];
So is our state: now here, now hence we passe[2]:
For Time attendes with shredding sithe for all,
   And Deathe at lengthe both oulde and yonge doth strike[3],
   And into dust dothe turne vs all alike.

Yet, if wee marke how swifte our race dothe ronne,
And waighe the cause, why wee created bee;
Then shall wee know, when that this life is donne,
Wee shall bee sure our countrie right to see.
   For here wee are but straungers, that must flitte[4]:
   The nearer home, the nearer to the pitte.

O happie they, that pondering this arighte,
Before that here their pilgrimage bee past,
Resigne this worlde, and marche with all their mighte
Within that pathe that leades where ioyes shall last[5];

---

[1] James i.   [2] Eccles. xiv.   [3] Isai. xl.
[4] 2 Cor. v.   [5] John xiv.

And whilst they maye, there treasure vp their
     store[1],
Where, without rust, it lastes for euermore.
This worlde must chaunge: that worlde shall still
     indure[2]:
Here pleasures fade; there shall they endlesse
     bee[3]:
Here man doth sinne; and there hee shal bee
     pure:
Here deathe hee tastes; and there shall neuer
     die[4]:
Here hath hee griefe; and there shall ioyes
     possesse[5],
As none hath seene, nor anie harte can gesse[6].

[1] Matt. vi.   [2] Rev. vi.   [3] Ib. xxi.
[4] 1 Cor. xv.   [5] Rev. xxi.   [6] 1 Cor. ii.

XVII.

HUMPHREY GIFFORD.

THE LIFE OF MAN

METAPHORICALLY COMPARED TO A SHIPPE SAYLING
ON THE SEAES IN A TEMPEST.

Haste homewardes, man; draw neerer to the
    shore:
The skies doe scowle, the windes doe blow amaine;
The raged rockes with rumbling noyse doe rore,
The foggie clowdes doe threaten stormes of raine;
Ech thing foreshowes a tempest is at hand;
Hoyst up thy sayles, and haste to happy land.

In worldly seaes thy silly ship is tost,
With waues of woe besette on euery side,
Blowne heere and there in daunger to bee lost:
Darke clowdes of sinne doe cause thee wander
    wide:
Unlesse thy God pitie some on thee take,
On rockes of rueth thou needes must shipwrack
    make.

Cut downe the mast of rancour and debate;
Unfraight the shippe of all vnlawfull wares;
Cast ouerboorde the packes of hoorded hate;
Pumpe out fowle vice, the cause of many cares;
If that some leeke it make thee stand in doubt,
Repentaunce serues to stoppe the water out.

Let God's pure word thy line and compasse bee;
And stedfast fayth vse thou in anckor's steede:
Lament thy sinnes; then shalt thou shortly see
That power diuine will helpe thee forth at neede.

Fell Sathan is chiefe rular of these seaes—
Hee seekes our wracke; hee doth these tempestes
    rayse.

In what wee may, let vs alwayes represse
The furious waues of lust and fond desire:
A quiet calme our conscience shall possesse,
If wee doe that which dutie doeth require:
By godly life in fine obtaine wee shall
The porte of blisse; to which God send vs all!

IN PRAISE OF THE CONTENTED MINDE.

IF all the ioyes that worldly wightes posesse
Were throughly scand, and pondred in their
    kindes,
No man of wit but iustly must confesse.
That they ioy most that haue contented mindes;
And other ioyes, which beare the name of ioyes,
Are not right ioyes, but sunneshines of anoyes.

In outward view we see a number glad,
Which make a shew as if mirth did abound,
When pinching grief within doth make them sad:
And many a one in these dayes may bee found,
Which faintly smile to shroud their sorowes so,
When oftentimes they pine in secreet woe.

But euery man that holdes himselfe content,
And yeeldes God thankes, as dutie doth require,
For all his giftes that hee to vs hath sent,
And is not vext with ouer great desire:
And such, I say, most quietly doe sleepe,
When fretting cares doth others waking keepe.

What doth auaile huge heapes of shining golde,
Or gay attyre, or stately buildinges braue,

If worldly pelfe thy heart in bondage holde?
Not thou thy goodes—thy goodes make thee
    their slaue.
For greedie men like Tantalus doe fare—
In midst of wealth they needie are and bare.

A warie heede that thinges go not to losse
Doth not amisse, so that it keepe the meane:
But still to toyle and moyle for worldly drosse,
And tast no ioy nor pleasure for our paine;
In carke and care both day and night to dwell,
Is nothing els but euen a very hell.

Wherefore, I say, as erst I did beginne,
Contented men enioy the greatest blisse:
Let vs content ourselues to flye from sinne,
And still abide what God's good pleasure is.
If ioy or paine, if wealth or want befall,
Let vs bee pleasde, and giue God thankes for all.

OF THE VANITIE OF THE WORLD.

As I lay musing in my bed
A heape of fancies came in head,
    Which greatly did molest mee;
Such sundry thoughtes of ioy and paine
Did meete within my pondring braine,
    That nothing could I rest mee.
Sometimes I felt exceeding ioy,
Sometimes the torment of annoy:
Euen now I laugh, euen now I weepe,
Euen now a slumber made mee sleepe.
Thus did I with thoughtes of straunge deuice
Lye musing alone in pensiue wise:
I knew not what meanes might health procure,
Nor finish the toyle I did indure;

And still I lay, and found no way
That best could make my cares decay.

Reuoluing these thinges in my minde,
Of wretched world the fancies blinde
   Alone awhile I ponder:
Which when I had perused well,
And saw no vertue there to dwell,
   It made me greatly wonder.
Is this that goodly thing, thought I,
That all men loue so earnestly?
Is this the fruit that it doth yeelde,
Whereby wee all are so beguilde?
Ah! Jesus, how then my heart did rue
Because I had folowed them as true!
Alas! wee haue lost the heauenly ioyes,
And haue beene deceaued with worldly toyes,
Whose fancies vaine will breede vs paine,
If Christ doe not restore againe.

O wretched man! leaue off therefore,—
In worldly thinges put trust no more,
   Which yeeldes nothing but sorow:
To God thy Lord with speede conuert,
Because thou most vncertain art
   If thou shalt liue to-morow.
Leaue of to quaffe, to daunce and play;
Remember still the iudgment-day:
Repent, relent, and call for grace,
For pardon aske whilst thou hast space.
Who doeth from his heart repentaunce craue,
Forgiuenes, saieth Christ, of mee shall haue.
Hee will not the death of a sinner giue,
But rather he should repent and liue.
Still laud the Lord; peruse his word,
And let thy deedes with it accord.

A LESSON FOR ALL ESTATES.

Hast thou desire thy golden dayes to spend
In blissfull state exempt from all annoyes?
So liue as if death now thy life should end;
Still treade the pathes that leade to perfect ioyes.
Bee slow to sinne, but speedie to ask grace:
How are they blest that thus runne out their race!

Ech night, ere sleepe shut vp thy drowsie eyes,
Thinke thou how much in day thou hast transgrest,
And pardon craue of God in any wise,
To doe that's good, and to forsake the rest.
Sinne thus shake of; the fiend for enuie weepes,
Sound are our ioyes, most quiet are our sleepes.

Haue not thy head so cloyd with worldly cares,
As to neglect that thou shouldst chiefly minde;
But beare an eye to Sathan's wily snares,
Who to beguile a thousand shiftes will finde.
Vaine are the ioyes that wretched world allowes:
Who trust them most doe trust but rotten bowes.

Shunne filthy vice; persist in doing well;
For doing well doth godly life procure;
And godly life makes vs with Christ to dwell
In endlesse blisse that euer shall endure.
Wee pray thee, Lord, our follyes to redresse,
That we thus doe, thus liue, this blisse possesse.

A GODLY DISCOURSE.

Like as the wight, farre banished from his soyle,
In countrey strange, opprest with grief and paine,
Doth nothing way his long and weary toyle,
So that he may come to his home againe;
And not accounts of perils great at hand,
For to attayne his owne desired land:

Such is the state of vs thy seruantes all,
Most gratious God, that here on earth do dwell:
We banisht were through Adam's cursed fall
From place of blisse euen to the pit of hell:
Our vice and sinnes as markes and signes wee haue,
Which still we beare, and shal doe to our graue.

When that all hope of remedy was past,
For our redresse when nothing could be founde,
Thine onely Sonne thou didst send downe at last
To salue this sore, and heale our deadly wounde:
Yet did they please to vse him as a meane
Us banisht wights for to call home agayne.

And for because thy Godhead thought it meete,
The sacred booke of thy most holy will
Thou didst vs leaue a lanterne to our feete,
To light our steppes in this our voyage still,
Directing vs what to eschew or take:
All this thou doest for vs vile sinners' sake.

Graunt vs sound fayth, that we take stedfast holde
On Christ his death, which did our raunsome pay;
So shall we shun the daungers manifold
Which would vs let, and cause vs run astray:
The wicked world, the flesh, the diuell, and all,
Are stumbling-blockes, ech howre to make vs fall.

This dungeon vile of Sathan is the nest,
A denne of dole, a sinke of deadly sinne.
Heauen is the hauen in which we hope to rest;
Death is the dore whereby we enter in.
Sweete Sauiour, graunt that so wee liue to die,
That after death we liue eternally.

THE COMPLAYNT OF A SINNER.

LIKE as the theefe in prison cast
  With wofull wayling mones,
When hope of pardon cleane is past,
  And sighes with dolefull grones:
So I a slaue to sinne,
  With sobs and many a feare,
As one, without thine ayde, forlorne,
  Before thy throne appeare.

O Lorde, in rage of wanton youth
  My follies did abounde,
And eke since that I knewe thy trueth
  My life hath beene vnsound:
Alas! I do confesse,
  I see the perfect way,
Yet frayltie of my feeble fleshe
  Doth make me run astray.

Aye me, when that some good desire,
  Woulde moue me to doe wel,
Affections fond make mee retire,
  And cause me to rebell.
I wake, yet am asleepe;
  I see, yet still am blinde;
In ill I runne with hedlong race;
  In good I come behinde.

Loe, thus in life I daily die,
  And dying shall not liue;
Vnlesse thy mercy speedily
  Some succour to me geue.
I die, O Lorde, I die!
  If thou doe mee forsake,
I shall be likened vnto those
  That fall into the lake.

When that one prop or onely stay
　　Holdes vp some house or wall,
If that the prop be tane away,
　　Needes must the building fall:
O Lorde, thou art the prop
　　To which I cleaue and leane:
If thou forsake or cast mee of,
　　I still shall liue in paine.

Although my hard and stony hart
　　Be apt to runne astray,
Yet let thy goodnesse mee conuert,
　　So shall I not decay:
Sweete God, doe rue my plaints,
　　And sheelde me from annoy:
Then my poore soule, this life once past,
　　Shall rest with thee in ioy.

A DREAME.

Layd in my quiet bed to rest,
When sleepe my senses all had drownd,
Such dreames arose within my breast,
As did with feare my minde confound.

Meethought I wandred in a woode,
Which was as darke as pitte of hell;
In midst of which such waters stoode,
That where to passe I could not tell.

The lion, tyger, wolfe, and beare,
There thundered forth such hideous cries,
As made huge eccoes in the aire,
And seemed almost to pearce the skies.

Long vext with care I there aboad,
And to get forth I wanted power:
At euery footstepe that I troad,
I feard some beast would mee deuoure.

Abyding thus, perplext with paine,
This case within myselfe I scand,
That humaine helpe was all in vaine,
Unlesse the Lord with vs doe stand.

Then falling flatte vpon my face,
In humble sorte to God I prayde,
That in this darke and dreadfull place
He would vouchsafe to bee mine ayde.

Arising, then a wight with winges,
Of auncient yeeres, meethinkes I see;
A burning torch in hand hee bringes,
And thus beganne to speake to me:

"That God whose ayd thou didst implore,
Hath sent mee hither for thy sake;
Pluck vp thy sprites, lament no more,
With mee thou must thy iourney take."

Against a huge and loftie hill
With swiftest pace meethinks wee go,
When such a sound mine eare did fill,
As moued my heart to bleede for woe.

Meethought I heard a woefull wight
In dolefull sorte powre forth great plaintes,
Whose cries did so my minde affright,
That euen with feare each member faintes.

"Fie!" quoth my guyd, "what meanes this change?
Passe on apace with courage bolde:
Hereby doth stand a prison strange,
Where wonderous thinges thou maiest beholde."

Then came we to a forte of brasse,
Where, peering through greate iron gates,
We saw a woman sit, alas!
Which ruthfully bewaylde her fates.

Her face was farre more white then snow,
And on her head a crowne shee ware,
Beset with stones, that glistered so
As hundred torches had bene there.

Her song was—"Woe! and weale away!
What torments here doe I sustayne!"
—A new mishap did her dismay,
Which more and more increast her payne.

An oggly creature, all in blacke,
Ran to her seate, and flung her downe:
Who rent her garments from her backe,
And spoyld her of her precious crowne.

This crowne he plaste vpon his hed,
And leauing her in dolefull case,
With swiftest pace away he fled,
And darknesse came in all the place.

* * * * * *

Then quoth my guyd: "Note well my talke,
And thou shalt heare this dreame declarde:
The wood, in which thou first didst walke,
Unto the worlde may be comparde.

The roaring beasts plainly expresse
The sundry snares in which we fall:
This gaole is named Deepe Distresse,
In which dame Virtue lies as thrall.

She is the wight, which heere within
So dolefully doth houle and crie:
Her foe is called Deadly Sinne,
That proffered here this villainie.

My name is Time, whom God hath sent
To warne thee of thy soule's decay :
In time therefore thy sinnes lament,
Least Time from thee be tane away."

As soone as he these wordes had sayd,
With swiftest pace away he flies;
And I thereat was so afrayde,
That drowsie sleepe forsooke mine eyes.

XVIII.

WILLIAM BYRD.

PSALME XV.

O Lord, who in thy sacred tent
  And holy hill shall dwell?
Euen he that both in heart and minde
  Dooth studie to do well.

In life vpright, in dealing iust,
  And he that from his heart
The truth doth speak with singlenes,
  All falshood set apart.

With tongue besides that hurts no man,
  By false and ill report;
Nor friends nor neighbours harme will doe
  Whereuer he resort.

That hates the bad, and loues the good,
  And faith that neuer breakes;
But keepes alwaies, though to his losse,
  The woord that once he speakes.

Nor filthy gaine by loue that seekes,
  Nor wealth so to possesse;
Nor that for bribes the guiltlesse soule
  Doth labour to oppresse.

Like as a mount, so shall he stand:
  Nothing shall him remoue,
That thus shall do, the Lord hath said;
  Nor man can it disproue.

PSALME XIII.

O Lord, how long wilt thou forget
    To send mee some reliefe?
For euer wilt thou hide thy face,
    And so increase my griefe?

How long shall I, with waxed heart,
    Seeke councell in my sprite?
How long shall my malicious foes
    Triumph, and me despite?

O Lord, my God, heare my complaint,
    Vttered with wofull breath;
Lighten mine eies; defend my life,
    That I sleep not in death:

Least that mine enemie say, I haue
    Against him, loe, preuayled:
At my downefall they will reioyce,
    That thus haue me assayl'd.

But in thy mercie, Lord, I trust,
    For that shall mee defend:
My hart doth ioy to see the help
    Which thou to mee wilt send.

Vnto the Lord, therefore, I sing,
    And doe lift vp my voyce;
And for his goodnesse shew'd to mee
    I will alway reioyce.

CARE FOR THY SOULE.

Care for thy soule as thing of greatest price,
Made to the end to tast of powre deuine,
Deuoide of guilt, abhorring sinne and vice,
Apt by God's grace to vertue to incline:

Care for it so, as by thy retchless traine
It not be brought to tast eternall paine.

Care for thy corps, but chiefly for soule's sake ;
Cut off excesse ; susteining food is best ;
To vanquish pride, but comely clothing take ;
Seeke after skill ; deepe ignorance detest :
Care so, I say, the flesh to feed and cloth,
That thou harme not thy soule and bodie both.

Care for the world to do thy bodie right ;
Racke not thy wit to winne by wicked waies ;
Seeke not to oppresse the weake by wrongfull
    might ;
To pay thy dew do banish all delayes :
Care to dispend according to thy store,
And in like sort be mindfull of the poore.

Care for thy soule, as for thy chiefest stay ;
Care for thy bodie, for the soule's auaile ;
Care for the world, for bodie's help alway ;
Care, yet but so as vertue may preuaile :
Care in such sort that thou be sure of this,—
Care keep thee not from heauen and heauenly
    blisse.

THE MARTIRS.

How do I vse my paper, ink, and pen,
And call my wits to counsel what to say !
Such memories were made for mortall men—
I speak of saintes, whose names cannot decaye :
An angel's trump were fitter for to sound
Their glorious death, if such on earth were found.

That store of such were once on earth pursu'd,
The histories of auncient times record,

THE MARTYRS.

Whose constancie great tirants' rage subdued,
Through patient death professing Christ their Lord:
As his apostles perfect witnesse bere,
With many more that blessed martirs were:

Whose patience rare and most couragious minde,
With fame renoun'd, perpetuall shall endure;
By whose examples we may rightly finde
Of holie life and death a patterne pure.
That we, therefore, their vertues may embrace,
Pray we to Christ to guide vs with his grace.

XIX.

ANTHONY MUNDAY.

A DITTIE

Declaring the uncertaintie of our earthly honor, the certaine account that we must all make of death; and therefore that we should make ourselues ready at all times, because we are ignorant of our latter howre.

WHAT state so sure but time subvarts?
　What pleasure that is voide of paine?
What cheereful change of former smarts
　But turnes straitwaie to greefe againe?
What credite may a man repose
　Vppon so fraile a clod of clay,
Which as to-day in sollace goes,
　To-morrow is brought to earthly bay?
　　　Thinke, O man!
How thy glasse is daily sette to runne,
And how thy life shall passe when it is doone:
Thy graue hath then thy glory wun,
And all thy pompe in cinders laide full lowe.
　　Take example
By the fragrant flower in the feeld,
Which as to-day in brauery is beheld,
The parching sun hath ouer-quel'd.
O wretched man! euen thou thyselfe art so.
　　How then?
How canst thou bragge, or canst thou boast,
　　　How that thou maiest
　　　Or that thou shalt
Enjoy thy life untill to-morrow day?

A DITTIE.

    Thou seest
That death subdues the strength of kings,
    Of high and lowe,
    Of rich and poore;
And all as one he dooth call awaie.

  * * * * * *

    To goe,
Put on your black aray; for needes you must away
Unto your house of clay:
Prepare your conscience gay against the dreadfull day,
    That you may be
Christ's chosen flocke and sheepe,
Whom he will safely keepe,
Whether you doo wake or sleepe:
    Then shall the hellish foe
    Away in terror goe,
    This joy to see.
Remember this, amidst your blisse,
 That Christ hath redeemed vs by his blood.
Then let vs kill our affections so ill,
 To be elected in his seruants' good.
Then shall we be sure for aye to endure
On God's right hand among the pure;
When as the ill against their will
The endlesse paine shall passe untill.
   God graunt us feruent constancie
   To auoide so great extremitie,
   That by his grace continuallie
   We may purchase heauen's felicitie!

A DITTIE

Which sheweth by example of diuers worthy personages past in ancient time, that neither strength, wit, beautie, riches, or any transitory things, wherein worldlings put any confidence, can saue them from the stroke of death.

ADIEW, my former pleasure,
  For 1 of force must leaue thee:
I see my state is most unsure,
  And thou hast long deceiude me.
Time bids me minde my latter end,
  And that I am but clay;
And euerie hour I doo offend
  In manie a wicked waie.
      Then farewell sinne,
      I will beginne
To sorrow for my wicked life at the last,
  And feare to sinne any more:
For when I remember all that is past,
  My hart doth bleede therefore.

I see that ualiant Sampson,
  Who uaunted of his stature,
His strength hath failde and he is gone;
  Time forst him yeeld to nature:
And all the courage he possesst
  Amidst his flowring dayes,
When death did call him home to rest,
  Did uade from him straitwaies.
      Then why should I
      On strength rely,
Perceiuing that the stoutest hart dooth obey,
  When death dooth shew his power?
And so must I needes (as all flesh) passe away;
  For strength is but a flower.

A DITTIE.

I see that wise king Salomon,
  Whose wisedome was most excellent,
Among the rest is dead and gone,
  For all his prudent gouernment.
And what is he that liueth now
  In wisedome most profound?
But death compelleth him to bow,
  And brings him to the ground.
        If strength then faile,
        And wit doth quaile,
Vnwise were I once for to think that I might
  Escape the stroke of death;
And know that there is on the earth no one right,
  But must resign his breath.

I see that faire young Absalon,
  Beautie did nought auaile him:
The welthy glutton eke is gone,
  His riches could not vaile him.
And he that had his barnes so thwakt,
  And bade his soul take rest,
In one night from his wealth was rapt,
  .And so was dispossest.
        Thus see you plain,
        It is in vaine
To make anie certaine account of this life,
  Or in yourselues to trust:
Therefore make you ready to part from this strife,
  For to the earth you must.

A DITTIE

*Wherein the brevitie of man's life is described, how soone his
pompe vanisheth away, and he brought to his latest home.*

The statelie pine, whose braunches spread so faire,
    By winde or weather wasted is at length;
The sturdie oake, that clymeth in the ayre,
    In time dooth lose his beautie and his strength;
The fayrest flower, that florisht as to-daie,
To-morrow seemeth like the withered haie.

So fare it with the present state of man,
    Whose showe of healthe dooth argue manie yeares:
But as his life is likened to a span,
    So suddaine sicknes pulles him from his peeres;
And where he seemde for longer time to-daie,
To-morrow lies he as a lumpe of clay.

The infant yong, the milk-white aged head,
    The gallant youth that braueth with the best,
We see with earth are quickly ouerspreade,
    And both alike brought to their latest rest:
As soone to market commeth to be solde
The tender lambe's skin as the weather's olde.

Death is not partiall, as the prouerb saies;
    The prince and peasant both with him are one:
The sweetest face that's painted now-a-daies,
    And highest head set forth with pearl and stone,
When he hath brought them to the earthly graue,
Beare no more reckoning then the poorest slaue.

The wealthy chuffe, that makes his gold his god,
    And scrapes and scratches all the mucke he may,
And with the world doth play at euen and od,
    When death thinks good to take him hence away,
Hath no more ritches in his winding-sheete
Then the poore soule that sterued in the streete.

Vnhappie man! that runneth on thy race,
  Not minding where thy crazed bones must rest:
But woe to thee that doost forget the place,
  Purchast for thee to liue amongst the blest!
Spend then thy life in such a good regard,
That Christe's blessing may be thy reward.

STANZAS

*From "The Complaint of Jonas," which forms a section
of "The Mirror of Mutabilitie."*

You therefore that remain on earth,
  Let this your minde suffise;
Feare still for to displease the Lord—
  Be not to worldly wise.

Fix stil your minde on heauenly things,
  That neuer wil decay—
The rest are but as shadows heer,
  And soone wil passe away.

What vantage is it for a man
  To haue of riches store,
And for to want the fear of God,
  Which stil should be before?

The more a man doth fixe his minde
  Vpon that filthy drosse,
The more endamaged is his soule
  Vnto the vtter losse.

For welth doth pamper him so much,
  That God is clene forgot,
And then at last vnto his pain
  Vpon him falls the lot;

So that all good and vertuous men
  From company refuse him,
And where before he was esteem'd,
  Now they disdain to vse him.

* * * * * * *

Turne vnto God, and God to you
  Wil turn his cheerful face;
Flye slauish sloth, and then be sure
  That God will you imbrace.

For idlenes is enemye
  To goodnes, as men say;
Therefore doo shun the enemye,
  And on the vertue stay.

Let all that haue you preter-past
  Examples be to you,
How you may learn in all assayes
  Vile sin for to eschew.

And thus if you direct your wayes,
  You walk the path so right,
That heauen is your inheritance
  In foyle of Sathan's spight.

XX.

SIR WALTER RALEIGH.

THE FAREWELL.

Goe, soule, the bodie's guest,
Vpon a thanklesse arrant:
Feare not to touch the best;
Thy truth shall be thy warrant:
   Goe, since I needs must dye,
   And giue them all the lye.

Say to the court, it glowes
And shines like painted wood;
Say to the church, it shewes
What's good, but does no good:
   If court and church reply,
   Then giue them both the lye.

Tell potentates, they liue
Acting, but oh! their actions
Not loued vnless they giue;
Nor strong but by affection:
   If potentates reply,
   Giue potentates the lye.

Tell men of high condition,
That manage the estate,
Their purpose is ambition,
Their practice onely hate;
   And if they once reply,
   Then giue them all the lye.

Tell those that braue it most,
They beg for more by spending,

Who in their greatest cost
Like nothing but commending:
    And if they make reply,
    Then giue them all the lye.

Tell Zeale it wants deuotion;
Tell Loue it is but lust;
Tell Time it meets but motion;
Tell Flesh it is but dust:
    And wish them not reply,
    For thou must giue the lye.

Tell Age it daily wasteth;
Tell Honour how it alters;
Tell Beauty how she blasteth;
Tell Fauour how it falters:
    And as they shall reply,
    Giue euery one the lye.

Tell Wit how much it wrangles
In fickle points of nicenesse:
Tell Wisdome she entangles
Herself in ouerwiseness:
    And when they doe reply,
    Straight giue them both the lye.

Tell Physicke of her boldnesse;
Tell Skill it is preuention;
Tell Charity of coldnesse;
Tell Law it is contention:
    And as they doe reply,
    Then giue them still the lye.

Tell Fortune of her blindnesse;
Tell Nature of decay;
Tell Friendship of vnkindnesse;
Tell Justice of delay:
    And if they will reply,
    Then giue them all the lye.

Tell Arts they haue no soundnesse,
But vary by esteeming;
Tell Schooles they want profoundnesse,
And stand so much on seeming:
  If Arts and Schooles reply,
  Giue Arts and Schooles the lye.

Tell Faith it's fled the citie;
Tell how the Countrey erreth;
Tell Manhood shakes off pitie;
Tell Vertue least preferreth:
  And if they doe reply,
  Spare not to giue the lye.

So, when thou hast, as I
Commanded thee, done blabbing;
Because to giue the lye
Deserues no lesse than stabbing;
  Stab at thee he that will,
  No stab thy soule can kill.

MY PILGRIMAGE.

Giue me my scallop-shell of quiet,
My staffe of faith to walk upon,
My scrip of ioye, (immortal diet!)
My bottle of saluation,
My gowne of glory, hope's true gage;
—And thus I take my pilgrimage.

Blood must be my body's balmer,
While my soule, like peaceful palmer,
Travelleth towards the land of heauen:
Other balm will not be giuen.
Over the silver mountains,
Where spring the nectar-fountains,
     There will I kiss
     The bowle of bliss,

And drink mine everlasting fill
Upon euery milken hill:
My soule will be adry before,
But after that will thirst no more.

*　　*　　*　　*　　*　　*　　*

AN EPITAPH.

(Said to have been written the night before his Execution.)

EUEN such is Time, which takes on trust
Our youth, and ioyes, and all we haue,
And payes us but with age and dust,
Which in the dark and silent graue,
When we have wandred all our wayes,
Shuts up the story of our dayes;
And from which earth, and graue, and dust,
The Lord shall raise me up, I trust.

XXI.

ABRAHAM FRAUNCE.

PSALM LXXII.

God, th' æternal God, noe doubt is good to the
  godly,
Giuing grace to the pure, and mercy to Israel
  holy:
And yet, alas! my feete, my faynte feet gan to be
  slyding,
And I was almost gone and fall'n to a dangerous
  error.
For my soul did grudg, my hart consumed in an-
  ger,
And myne eyes disdayng'd, when I saw that such
  men abounded
With wealth, health, and joy, whose myndes with
  myschif abounded,
Theyr body stowt and strong, theyr lyms still
  lyuely apearing,
Neyther feare any panges of death, nor feele any
  sicknes:
Some still mourne, they laughe: some lyue un-
  fortunate euer,
They for ioy doe triumphe, and taste aduersity
  neuer;
Which makes them with pryde, with scornful
  pryde to be chayned,
And with blood-thirsting disdaigne as a roabe to
  be cou'red.

* * * * * * *

Tush! say they, can God from the highest heauens
    to the lowest
Earth vouchsaulf, thinck you, those prince-like
    eyes be bowing?
'Tis but a vaine conceipt of fooles to be fondly
    referring
Euery jesting trick and trifling toy to the
    Thundrer:
For loe these be the men whoe rule and reign
    with aboundance;
These, and who but these? Why then, what
    meane I to lift up
Cleane handes and pure hart to the heu'ns? what
    meane I to offer
Praise and thanksgeuing to the Lord? what meane
    I to suffer
Such plagues with patience? Yea, and almost
    had I spoken
Euen as they did speake, which thought noe God
    to be guyding.
But soe should I, alas! haue iudged thy folk to be
    luckless,
Thy sons forsaken, thy saints vnworthily haples.
Thus did I thinck and muse, and search what
    might be the matter:
But yet I could not, alas! conceaue so hidden a
    woonder,
Vntil I left myself, and all my thoughts did
    abandon,
And to thy sacred place, to thy sanctuary, lastly
    repayred.
There did I see, O Lord, these men's vnfortunate
    endings;
Endings mute, and fit for their vngodly beginnings.
Then did I see how they did stand in slippery
    places,

Lifted aloft, that their downefalling might be the greater.
Lyving Lord, how soone is this theyr glory triumphant
Dasht, confounded, gone, drownd in destruction endless!
Their fame's soone outworne, theyr names extinct in a moment,
Lyke to a dreame, that lyues by a sleep, and dyes with a slumber.
—Thus my soule did greeue, my hart did languish in anguish;
Soe blynde were myne eyes, my minde soe plunged in error,
That noe more than a beast did I know this mystery sacred.
Yet thou heldst my hande, and kepst my soule from the dungeon;
Thou didst guyde my feete, and me with glory receauedst.
For what in heau'n or in earth shall I loue, or woorthyly wonder,
But my most good God, my Lord and mighty Jehova?
Though my flesh oft faint, my hart's oft drowned in horror,
God neuer fayleth, but will be my mighty protector.
Such as God forsake, and take to a slippery comfort,
Trust to a broken staffe, and taste of woorthy reuengement.
In my God, therefore, my trust is wholly reposed,
And his name wil I praise, and sing his glory renowmed.

XXII.

JOHN DAVIES.

SONETS.

I.

If in a three-square glasse, as thick as cleare,
(Being but dark earth, though made diaphanall)
Beauties diuine, that rauish, seme appeare,
Making the soule with ioy in trance to fall;
What then, my soule, shalt thou in heau'n behold,
In that cleare mirror of the TRINITY?
What though it were not that it could be told?
For 'tis a glorious yet dark mistery!
It is *that* which is furthest from description,
Whose beaming beauty's more then infinite:
It's glorie's monument, whose superscription
Is, *Here lies Light,* alone indefinite:
  Then, O light limitlesse, let me, poore me,
  Still liue obscure, so I may still see thee.

II.

Were manne's thoughts to be measured by daies,
Ten thousand thoughts ten thousand daies should haue,
Which in a day the mynd doth daily raise;
For still the mind's in motion like a waue:
Or should his daies be measured by thought,
Then times shortst moment they would faster flee:
Yet thought doth make his life both long and nought—
That's nought if longe, and longe if nought it bee!
If longe it bee, for being nought, though short,

The shortest thought of longe life is too longe,
Which thinkes it longe in laboure, short in sport;
So thought makes life to be still old, or yonge:
　But sith its full of thought, sith full of synnes,
　Think it may ende, as thought of it beginnes.

III.

Whiles in my soule I feel the soft warme hand
Of grace, to thaw the frozen dregs of sin,
She, angell arm'd, on Eden's walls doth stand,
To keep out outward ioyes that would come in.
But when that holy hand is tane away,
And that my soule congealeth, as before,
She outward comfort seeks with care each way,
And runs to meet them at each sence's door.
Yet they but at the first sight only please;
They shrink, or breed abhorr'd satiety.
But diuine comforts, far vnlike to these,
Do please the more, the more they stay and be.
　Then outward ioyes I inwardly detest,
　Sith they stay not, or stay but in vnrest.

IV.

True loue is Charity begun to be,
Which is when Loue beginneth to be true;
But to the high'st growes louing Charity,
When she the High'st alone doth loue to view.
O Charity! that euermore doost flame
In that dread Maiestie's eternall brest,
When by thy heate shall my loue lose hir name,
And made to flame, like thee, in restlesse rest?
Well-featured flesh too base a subiect is
For sour'raign loue's diuine ay blest imbrace:
The loue of flesh loues nought but flesh; but this
Loues nought that sauors of a thing so base.
　Then be the priest, and as an host I'le dy,
　Offerd to heau'n in flames of Charity.

V.

The ofter sinne, the more griefe, shewes a saint;
The ofter sinne, the less griefe, notes a fiend:
But oft with griefe to sinne the soule doth taint;
And oft to sinne with ioy the soule doth rend.
To sinne on hope is sinne most full of feare;
To sinne of malice is the diuel's sinne:
One is that Christ may greater burden beare,
The other, that his death might still beginne.
To sinne of frailtie is a sinne but weake;
To sinne in strength the stronger makes the blame:
The first the reed Christ bare hath powre to breake,
The last his thornie crowne can scarce vnframe:
 But, finally, to sinne malitiously,
 Reed, crowne, nor crosse, hath power to crucifie.

VI.

A righteous man still feareth all his deeds,
Lest done for feare or in hypocrisie:
Hypocrisie, as with the corne doe weeds,
Still growes vp with faith, hope, and charitie.
But it bewraies they are no hypocrites,
That most of all hypocrisie doe feare:
For who are worst of all in their owne sights,
In God's deere sight doe best of all appeare.
To feare that we nor loue nor feare aright
Is no lesse perfect feare, than rightest loue:
And to suspect our steps in greatest light
Doth argue, God our hearts and steps doth moue:
 But right to run, and feare no whit at all,
 Presageth we are neere a fearefull fall.

VII.

In th' act of sinne the guilt of conscience
Doth spoile our sport, sith our soules fainting
  bleed;

For that worme feeds vpon our inward sense
More than sinne's manna outward sense doth feed:
But he on whom God's glorious face doth shine,
The more his griefes, the more his ioyes abound;
For who are drunke with diuine pleasures' wine
Can feele no torments which the senses wound.
Then 'tis a torment nere to be tormented
In vertue's cause, nor for sinne's fowle default:
And no worse tempting, than nere to be tempted;
For we must peace attaine by sinne's assault.
  Then blessed is the crosse that brings the crowne,
  And glorious is the shame that gaines renowne.

GOD ETERNAL.

COULD he beginne, Beginnings that began?
If so he could, what is beginninglesse?
Or Time, or Nothing. That's vntrue; for than,
If there were Time, it was not motionlesse;
For Time is made by Motion, all confesse:
But where there Nothing is, no Motion is:
For Nothing hath no motion, and much lesse
Can Nothing make of nothing Something. This
Something sometime of nothing made all is.

God euer was, and neuer was not God:
Not made by Nothing: nothing could him make.
Could Nothing make and not make? This is odde;
And so is he that could creation take
Of nothing: for all was, when as he spake;
Nothing was made that was not made by it:
Then nothing was that could it vndertake;
To make its Maker what had powre or wit?
Not him that can doe all that he thinkes fit.

Time's but a moment's flux, and measured
By distance of two instants: this we proue,

Which then commenced, itselfe considered,
When first the orbs of heauen began to moue;
That but sixe thousand yeeres, not much aboue.
But what's so many yeeres as may be cast
In thrice as many ages, to remoue
Eternitie from being fixed fast,
And God therein from being first and last.

He is eternall; what is so, is He:
So is no creature, for it once was made:
Then ere it could be made it could not be.
But the Creator euer beeing had,
To pull out from Not being: who can wade
(Beeing a deapth so infinite profound)
But he that was, and is, and cannot fade,
This Beeing infinite, this deapth most sound,
To lift vp all to Beeing, there beeing dround?

Eternity and Time are opposite;
For time no more can bound eternity,
Then Finite can invirone Infinite;
Both of both which haue such repugnancy,
As nere can stand with God's true unity:
Eternity is then produced from hence—
By ioyning of his sole Infinite
With his essentiall intelligence;
And all the attributes proceed from thence.

If then eternity doth bound this One,
Or rather he bounds all Eternity,
How could he bee? or beeing all alone,
How could he worke, that works vncessantly,
(For hee's all act that acts continually,)
Hauing no subiect whereupon to worke?
And beeing without his creatures vtterly,
It seemes he must in desolation lurke,
Which must of force an actiue nature irke.

THOSE BLESSED WHO ENDURE TEMPTATION.

How neede the soule to stand vpon her guard,
And keep the tempter at the sp'rit's sword point!
Else pride will puffe her, sith so well she far'd,
Which swelling will runne downe from ioynt to
  ioynt,
That she will burst, if grace her not annoynt.
This found he true, that found this true repast
In the third heau'n, as God did fore-appoint:
Yet must he buffets with such banquets taste,
Lest he should be puft vp, and so disgrac'd.

For our soule's foe extracts ill out of good,
As our soule's friend doth draw good out of ill.
The foe can foile, if he be not withstood,
With pride our piety and our good-will.
But our best friend, though we offend him still,
From these offences drawes humilitie;
Which makes vs crouch, and kneele, and pray,
  vntill
He doth commiserate our misery:
This doth our friend, vnlike our enemie.

The soule cannot her fondnesse more bewray,
Then when she doth temptations strong resist:
For like as when our pulses strongly play,
We know we neede not then a Galenist;
So when the soule doth paint, striue, and persist
In strugling with temptations, then we kno
That soule with perfect health is truly blest:
For she by demonstration it doth sho;
And blest are all those soules that striueth so.

HEAUENLY MANSIONS.

Sith God is euer changlesse as hee's good,
We wormes most mutable in spight of change
May euer stand in him that euer stood,
By faith, and hope, and love; and neuer range
But when through him we go to places strange.
And though by nature mutable we be,
Yet may his grace from vs that state estrange,
And match vs to immutability
In the bride-chamber of feliecity.

Hee's true of promise, sith he cannot change;
Then why should sorrowing synners feare to dye?
Since earth's familiars are to heauen strange,
Then heauen we cannot haue while here we lye.
And he that's free from all vncertainty
Hath in his euer neuer-failing word
Giu'n vs by deede, with his bloud seald, an hie
And heauenly mantion, which he doth afford
To all whose wills do with his will accord.

The euer-liuing God, sole Lord of life,
He was and is from all eternity:
If he be such a husband, shall his wife,
Or any member of her, fear to dye
In him with whom is immortality?
Hee's life itselfe; then of himself he moues,
And all his members moues immediately
To rest in him: the rest from him he 'moues:
So all moues by him which he hates or loues.

DIUINE MERCY AS GREAT AS GOD'S DIUINITY.

How far that mercy reacheth, erst we toucht:
Then needlesse were it eft to handle it:
As pow'rfull as himselfe we it auoucht,
And hee's omnipotent: then, if it fit
His pow'r, it is at least most infinit!
Which attribute of his Omnipotence,
That most is mentioned in holy writ,
Is the firm pillar of our confidence,
Sith it to grace hath euer reference.

Almightinesse includeth whatsoere
That is most absolutlie good or great:
Then its the prop that all in all doth beare;
More then most actiue in each glorious feate,
Which by still actiue good doth ill defeate.
Though it seemd passiue when in flesh 'twas shown,
Yet in the flesh that passion had her seate:
God's a pure act, which ne're was passiue known,
Who made that flesh he tooke, and held his owne.

GOD'S GLORY AND GOODNES INEXPLICABLE.

This wondrous Trinity in Vnity
Is vnderstood to bee: but how? And here
Is such a gulph of deepest mistery
As none, without bee'ng quite orewhelmd with fear,
Can looke therein to tell the secrets there!
For what beseeming that good evriething
Can we imagin, though we angels were?
That is as farre past all imagining
As we are short of paceing with his wing.

We erre in nought with danger more extreame,
Nor in ought labour with more hard assay;
Yet nought we know with more hart's ioy than
    them:
But in their search, if once we lose our way,
We may be lost and vtterly decay:
Its deadly dangerous then for them to looke
Through waies more sullen then the foe of day,
Without Faith's lanthorne, Truth's most blessed
    booke,
Which none ere left, but straight the way forsooke.

For Justice' Sonne was sent by Grace his sire
The gospell to promulgate from his brest,
His councels to disclose, our doubts to chere:
Then if we go to seeke this Beeing blest
Without these helpes, we strayeng neuer rest.

*   *   *   *   *

GRIEFE FOR SINNE IS A IOYFULL SORROW.

But yet the good which we by sinne receaue
Doth farre surmount the ill that comes from thence.
If God the world of ill should quite bereaue,
There were no test to try our sapience;
So might want reason and intelligence:
But we haue both, to know the good from bad;
So know we God, and our soule's safe defence:
Then since by ill we are so well bestad,
We cannot greeue for ill, but must be glad.

For were there no temptation, then no fight;
And if no fight, no victory could be:
No victory, no palmes nor vertues white;
No crosse, no crowne of immortality:
And thus from ill comes good abundantly:

For by the conquest of it we are crown'd
With glory in secure felicity.
So from great ills more goods to vs redound,
As oft most sicknesse maketh vs most sound.

Ill, like a mole vpon the world's faire cheeke,
Doth stil set forth that fairenes much the more:
She were to seeke much good were ill to seeke,
For good by ill increaseth strength and store,
At least in our conceit, and vertuous lore.
There's nought so euill that is good for nought:
God giuing vs a salue for ev'ry sore,
The good are humbled by their euil'st thought:
So to the good al's good that ill hath wrought.

BLESSED BE THE MERCIFULL: FOR THEY SHALL OBTAINE MERCY.

(Matt. v. 7.)

WHAT wit hath man to leaue that wealth behind,
Which he might carry hence when hence he goes?
What almes he giues aliue, he, dead, doth find;
But what he leaues behind him, he doth lose.
To giue away then is to beare away;
They most do hold who haue the openest hands:
To hold too hard makes much the lesse to stay;
Though stay there may more then the hand commands.
The beggar's belly is the batful'st ground
That we can sow in; for it multiplies
Our faith and hope, and makes our loue abound,
And what else grace and nature deerely prize:
  So thus may kings be richer in their graue
  Then on their thrones, though all the world they haue.

STANZAS

From " Christ's Crosse, containing Christ Crucified, described in speaking picture."

(*The author, having described the agony of our Lord, thus proceeds to address Nature.*)

O NATURE, carefull mother of vs all,
How canst thou liue to see thy God thus die?
To heare his paines, thus, thus for pittie call,
And yet to find no grace in pittie's eie!
    Thy frame, deere Nature, should be quite dissolu'd,
    Or thy whole powers into teares resolu'd.

His anguish hauing this in silence said,
See now how he sore labours for the last:
The last deneere of sinne's debt being defraid,
It now remains that Death the reckning cast:
    But heauy Death, because the summe is great,
    Takes yet some longer time to doe the feat.

But now, my soule, here let vs make a station,
To view perspicuously this sad aspect:
And through the Jacob's staffe of Christ his passion
Let's spie with our right eie his paines' effect:
    That in the lab'rinth of his languishment
    We may, though lost therein, find solagement.

The mind, still crost with heart-tormenting crosses,
Here finds a crosse to keepe such crosses out:
Here may the loser find more than his losses,
If Faith beleeue what here Faith cannot doubt:
    For all his wounds with voice vociferant
    Crie out they can more than supply each want.

This holy crosse is the true Tutament,
Protecting all ensheltered by the same;

And though Disaster's face be truculent,
Yet will this engine set it fair in frame:
   This is the feeble soule's nere-failing crouch,
   And grieued bodies hard but wholesom'st couch.

Looke on this crosse, when thou art stung with care;
It cures forthwith like Moises' metl'd snake:
What can afflict thee when thy passions are
Pattern'd by his, that paines perfections make?
   Wilt be so God-vnlike, to see thy God
   Embrace the whip, and thou abhorre the rod?

See, see, the more than all soule-slaying paines,
Which more than all for thee and all he prou'd:
What man, except a God he be, sustaines
Such hels of paine for man with mind unmou'd?
   What part, as erst was said, of all his parts,
   But tortur'd is with smarts, exceeding smarts?

His vaines and nerues, that channelize his blood,
By violent conuulsions all confracted;
His bones and ioynts, from whence they whilome stood,
With rackings quite disloked and distracted:
   His head, hands, feet, yea, all from top to toe,
   Make but the imperfect corpse of perfect woe.

O that mine head were head of seau'nfold Nyle,
That from the same might flowe great floods of teares,
Therein to bathe his bloodlesse body, while
His blood effuz'd, in sight confuz'd appeares!
   Then should my teares egelidate his gore,
   That from his blood founts for me flow'd before.

O burning loue! O large and lasting loue!
What angel's tongue thy limits can describe?

That dost extend thyself all loue aboue,
For which all praise loue ought to thee ascribe:
   Sith skarce the tongue of God's humanitie
   Can well describe this boundlesse charitie.

Why do I liue? alas, why do I liue?
Why is not my heart loue-sicke to the death?
But shall I liue my louing Lord to grieue?
O no! O rather let me lose my breath:
   Then take me to thee, Loue; O let me die,
   Onely but for thy loue, and sinne to flie.

Stay me with flagons; with fruit comfort me;
Now I am sicke, heart-sicke of sweetest loue:
Then let me liue, sweet Loue, alone in thee,
For loue desires in that Belou'd to moue:
   I liue and moue in thee, but yet, O yet,
   I liue to mone; that is, to make thee fret.

   *   *   *   *   *   *   *

O let the summe of all be all, and some,
Comprised in thy heau'n-surmounting praise:
Thou wast, and art, and shalt be aye to come,
The subiect of thy subiects' thankfull laies;
   Who with aduanced voice doe carroll forth
   The praise of thine inestimable worth.

And sith thy soule for me is so conflicted,
My soule to thee in griefes shall be affected:
And, for thy flesh through loue is so afflicted,
My flesh for thy high loue shall be deiected:
   Soule, flesh, and spirit, for thy spirit, flesh, and
     soule,
   Shall longing pine in flesh-repining dole.

Mine onely schoole shall be mount Caluerie;
The pulpit but the crosse; and teacher none,
But the mere crucifixe to mortifie;
No letters but thy blessed wounds alone:

No commaes but thy stripes; no periods
But thy nailes, crowne of thornes, speare, whips,
    and rods.

None other booke but thy vnclasped side,
Wherein's contain'd all skils angelical:
None other lesson but Christ crucified
Will I ere learne; for that is all in all:
    Wherein selfe curiositie may find
    Matter to please the most displeased mind.

Here, by our Master's nakednesse, we learne
What weeds to weare; by his thorne-crowned head,
How to adorn vs; and we may discerne
By his most bitter gall, how to be fed:
    How to reuenge, by praying for his foes;
    And, lying on his crosse, how to repose.

For when we read him ouer, see we shall
His head with thornes, his eares with blasphemies,
His eies with teares, his honnied mouth with gall,
With wounds his flesh, his bones with agonies,
    All full: and yet with all to heare him say,
    So man might liue, he would thus languish aye!

THE DEATH OF CHRIST.

Now hath the great Creator, for man's sake,
The second Adam cast into a sleepe:
Whiles of his heart-blood hee his spouse doth make,
For whom his heart doth blood and water weepe:
    Which compound teares are turn'd to ioy intire;
    For his heart-blood effects his heart's desire.

Which deere desire was our deere spouse to haue,
To be co-partner of his griefes and ioyes;

Which when he wooke his God vnto him gaue,
To comfort him in comforts and annoies;
    Which when he saw, he held (most faire to se!)
    Flesh of his flesh, bone of his bones, to be!

Now hath the monster, flesh-devouring Death,
Got him within his bowels: but though dead,
Looke how a woman groaning languisheth
In childbirth till shee be delivered:
    So groaneth Death, who trauelleth in paine,
    Till of his charge he be discharg'd again.

    *   *   *   *   *

O! that all spirits of high intelligence,
By royall armies, would themselues immure
In my blunt braines; that by their confluence
I might expresse with nectar'd phrases pure
    The praise that to this passion right pertaines,
    Whose sacred vertue sacred vertue staines!

The vertue of this passion is of pow'r
Reuenges red to change to mercies white:
This passion's vertue is so passing pure,
That fowle to faire it turnes, and darke to light:
    The landmarke to true rest, when troubles tosse
    In sorrowes' seas, is Christ vpon the crosse.

Ye vnconfused orders angellick,
In order come to take this blood effuz'd.
Bring forth celestiall bowles, with motion quick,
To which this pretious blood may be infuz'd:
    Let not one drop be lost of such rare blood,
    That makes men passing bad exceeding good.

Couer this *Aqua uitæ* with your wings
From touch of infidels and Jewes prophane:
They haue no interest in this King of kings,
Whose blood they suck'd, which blood will be
    their bane:

Make much thereof, sith but the least drop of it
Is worth ten thousand worlds for price and profit.

Yet let poore-spirited conuerts drinke their fill,
And swill their drie soules till with it they swell:
Such diuine surfetting is wholesome still;
For noysome humors it doth quite expell.
    Yea, though with griefe they swell and breake
        with paine,
    Such griefe brings ioy, and makes them whole
        againe.

The elephants of yore, inur'd to warre,
Before the fight some blood were vsed to see,
Which them incenst, the more to make them dare:
Then if a beast shall not our better be,
    Sith Christ wee see quite drown'd thus in his
        blood,
    We must endure the racke as he the rood.

Fine founts he opens, whence doe gushing flow
Red seas to drowne our blacke Egyptian sinnes,
That they no more may seeke our ouerthrow:
Then should we goe, like Israell's denizens,
    Through wasts of woes, orethrowing eu'ry let,
    Till we into the Land of Promise get.

XXIII.

THOMAS HOWELL.

THE OFFICE OF THE MINDE.

The office of the minde is to haue power
Uppon the bodye, and to order well
The body's office yeke in euery hower:
It is of the minde to lerne the perfite skyll,
The vayne desyers that rise him by to kill,
Wherby the mynde dothe kepe his perfite strength,
And yeke the bodye vanquishe loste at length.

Now where the minde is drowned with desyre
Of suche delyhtis as to the body longe,
The boddy then moste nedes consume with fyer
Of raging lustes a boute the same thronge;
So that the minde is cause of bothe ther wronge,
To put it selfe out of the proper place,
And bring the bodye to so euel a case.

For thus the minde, that oughte of righte to be
The teacher of the bodye to do well,
Doth make the same to euery euill agre,
Procuringe that it shoulde of right expell,
Wherby in bothe a mouinge blinde doth dwell;
Euen as within Narcyssus dyd remayne,
That through his shadowe to be soche agayne.

www.ingramcontent.com/pod-product-compliance
Lightning Source LLC
Chambersburg PA
CBHW071957220426
43662CB00009B/1168